AZTEC & MAYA
LIFE IN AN ANCIENT CIVILIZATION

AZTEC & MAYA
LIFE IN AN ANCIENT CIVILIZATION

THE EVERYDAY WORLD OF THE AZTECS, MAYA AND OTHER NATIVE CIVILIZATIONS OF
CENTRAL AMERICA AND MEXICO, WITH OVER 500 PHOTOGRAPHS AND FINE ART IMAGES

CHARLES PHILLIPS • CONSULTANT: DR DAVID M JONES

HERMES
HOUSE

CONTENTS

INTRODUCTION

On Good Friday, 21 April 1519, an expedition of 600-odd adventurers from the Spanish colony of Cuba dropped anchor off the beaches of San Juan de Ulúa, on the Gulf coast of Mexico, close to where the port of Veracruz would later be established. Under the command of Hernán Cortés, the men came ashore with their horses and exchanged gifts with the Totonac inhabitants of the region. About 300km (200 miles) inland, in the capital of the Aztec empire, the *tlatoani* (ruler) Moctezuma II received reports of the fair-skinned sailors, of the ships – which the trader-spies who were his informants saw as mountains floating on the sea – and of the Spanish cavalry or 'man-beasts'.

The landing in 1519 was not the first meeting between Europeans and the peoples of what became modern Mexico and Guatemala. There had been a number of brief encounters, including one in 1502

Below: Chacmools *received offerings of human hearts. This* chacmool *stood before the temple to Tláloc in Tenochtitlán.*

between Christopher Columbus and traders from the lands of the Aztecs' Maya neighbours. Yet this momentous day in 1519, which was the first step in an invasion that would bring the Aztec empire to its knees, inaugurated the first prolonged contact between two very different and essentially alien cultures: the European and the Mesoamerican.

MANY CIVILIZATIONS

Human activity in the region of Mexico and neighbouring Guatemala dates back 20,000 years or more, to the time when the first hunter-gatherers settled in the area. In the period between that time and the height of the Aztec empire, in the 14th–16th centuries AD, a number of civilizations rose and fell in the locality.

Historians apply the name 'Mesoamerica' both to these civilizations and to the area in which they arose. This ran southwards from the desert regions of north-central Mexico, then eastwards to include the Isthmus of Tehuantepec, the Yucatán peninsula, Guatemala, Honduras, western Nicaragua and north-western

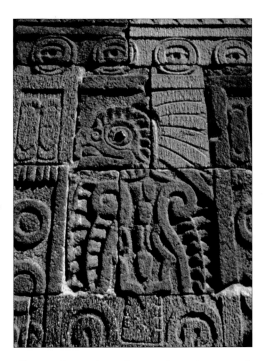

Above: A carving of an enigmatic quetzal-butterfly adorns the elegant Quetzalpapálotl Palace in Teotihuacán.

Costa Rica. Among these civilizations were the Olmecs, carvers of magnificent stone monuments and creators of a vast trading network in the 2nd millennium BC; the Zapotecs, builders of a mountaintop settlement at Monte Albán in Oaxaca, who may have been the first people in the region to develop written communication c.500BC; and the builders of the mysterious monumental city of Teotihuacán in highland Mexico c.100BC–c.AD500, who excelled in trade, the manufacture of enigmatic masks and the painting of evocative murals.

Others included the Maya, who in the period c.AD250–900 raised magnificent temples and palaces in the jungles of Guatemala and in parts of eastern Mexico, and who continued to thrive until the Spanish Conquest; the militaristic Toltecs, who built their capital Tollán north-west of Teotihuacán c.AD950 and developed bloodthirsty religious rites involving human sacrifice; the Mixtecs, who succeeded the Zapotecs in Oaxaca and

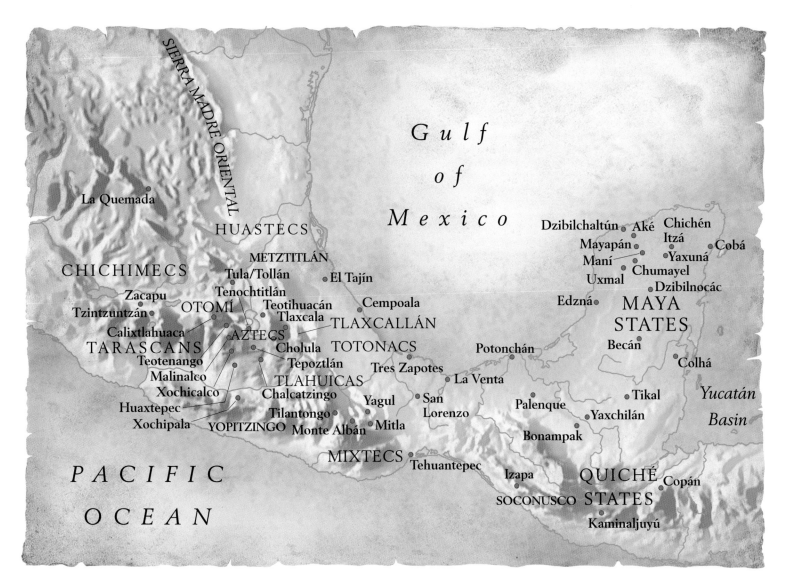

SIERRA MADRE ORIENTAL

La Quemada

HUASTECS

CHICHIMECS

METZTITLÁN

Tula/Tollán

El Tajín

Zacapu

Tenochtitlán

OTOMÍ

Teotihuacán

Cempoala

Tzintzuntzán

Tlaxcala

TLAXCALLÁN

Calixtlahuaca

AZTECS

Cholula

TOTONACS

Potonchán

TARASCANS

Teotenango

Tepoztlán

Tres Zapotes

La Venta

Malinalco

TLAHUICAS

Xochicalco

Chalcatzingo

Yagul

San

Huaxtepec

Tilantongo

Lorenzo

Xochipala

YOPITZINGO

Monte Albán

Mitla

MIXTECS

Tehuantepec

PACIFIC

OCEAN

Gulf

of

Mexico

Dzibilchaltún

Aké

Chichén

Itzá

Mayapán

Cobá

Maní

Yaxuná

Chumayel

Uxmal

Dzibilnocác

Edzná

MAYA

STATES

Becán

Colhá

Tikal

Yucatán

Palenque

Basin

Yaxchilán

Bonampak

Izapa

QUICHÉ

Copán

SOCONUSCO

STATES

Kaminaljuyú

who excelled in metalworking and hand-painted screenfold books; the Tarascans of Michoacán in western Mexico, highly skilled metalworkers who forged an empire after 1200; and the México, or Aztecs, who in the years after founding their capital of Tenochtitlán in 1325 built a vast empire encompassing 150,000sq km (58,000sq miles).

ALIEN CULTURES

Both the Mesoamericans and the Spanish invaders found plenty to marvel at and to disapprove of in the behaviour of their opponents. For example, it would appear that the Mesoamericans were shocked by the poor hygiene of the Spaniards. The conquistadors' accounts of the invasion tell of many occasions on which the locals doused them with incense. The invaders took this as a mark of respect, but historians suspect that the nobles of Tenochtitlán, who kept themselves very

Above: Mesoamerican cultural sites ranged over the years from San Lorenzo to Tenochtitlán and over miles from Tikal to La Quemada.

clean, were attempting to keep the stench of the unwashed soldiers at bay. On the other hand, the Spanish conquistadors were both attracted and repelled by what they found in Tenochtitlán when, after marching inland, allying with locals in Tlaxcala and defeating the lords of Cholula, they entered the Aztec capital on 7 November 1519.

The conquistadors were captivated by the beauty of the vast city laid out on islands in Lake Texcoco, by the elegance of the palaces and gardens inhabited by the ruler and nobility and by the astonishing range of goods for sale in the city's vast

Right: Aztec pilgrims took this greenstone mask from Teotihuacán and offered it in the Templo Mayor, Tenochtitlán.

market. However, they were equally shocked by the temples and ceremonial areas laid out to celebrate rites of human sacrifice, by the sight of priests with blood-matted hair and smoke-blackened skin, by images of Aztec gods and by blood-spattered reclining stone figures known as *chacmools* into which the still-warm hearts of sacrificial victims were placed.

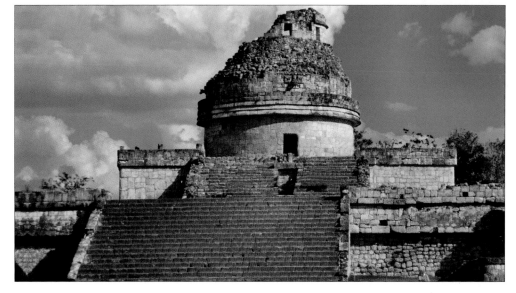

CULTURE CLASH

The Spanish did encounter certain elements familiar from their own European culture. As in Europe, the warriors' achievements were lauded and military might enforced political power, networks of trade and tribute were vibrant and a strong sense of the sacred informed all parts of life. However, other elements of Mesoamerican civilization were bafflingly strange or broke European taboos. For example, while the conquistadors were certainly not unfamiliar with torture and slaughter, nor squeamish about the sight of blood or even the display of prisoners' remains, they were unprepared for the Aztecs' ritual celebration of slaughter, in which human hearts were torn out as a key element of public religious ritual. They were shocked by the vast numbers of victims sacrificed and by the gods and goddesses honoured. They were horrified to learn that certain Aztec religious rites included cannibalism. Nobles and priests shared the flesh of victims who had earlier been sacrificed on the steps before the temple and whose hearts were displayed on the *chacmool*.

This cannibalistic rite was informed by the Aztecs' understanding that a sacrificial victim impersonated and finally became the god to whom he was sacrificed. The elite members of Aztec society admitted to the feast were thus able to share in the divine essence. Aztec worshippers frequently understood several distinct performers of and elements in ritual to share the identity of a god or goddess. This included priests and victims dressed in honour of deities as well as natural elements used in dedication or worship. At the blessing of a new aqueduct carrying water into Tenochtitlán during the reign of the Aztec *tlatoani* (ruler) Ahuítzotl (1486–1502), priests, dressed in the jade skirt associated with the water goddess Chalchiúhtlicue, offered incense and precious turquoise (a stone linked to the goddess) as the aqueduct was opened and the waters ran for the first time. The goddess, the priests dressed as the goddess, the turquoise and the water itself were all understood to be one in a concept typical of Mesoamericans but different to Western thought.

CYCLES OF TIME

Another key element of Mesoamerican culture that was immediately alien to the Europeans was the idea that the gods made time move in cycles. The Aztecs believed that the current world was the fifth in a succession of creations and that, within the current world age, events were destined to be repeated in a way which followed large, cyclical patterns.

Mesoamericans had a very deep respect for the past. In both Aztec and Maya lands, worshippers made respectful journeys to the great cities built by their ancestors such as Teotihuacán and Tollán for the Aztecs and Tikal and Chichén Itzá for the Maya. Indeed, the desire to recreate in the present the glories of the past was one of the driving forces behind the Aztec empire. The Aztecs wanted to honour the achievements of the Toltec founders of Tollán. They were also keen to celebrate the sacred city of Teotihuacán, which they viewed as the birthplace of the gods. Here, according to Aztec religious narrative, on the very ground and before the very buildings still visible today, the gods had gathered in the primordial past to create the sun and moon and set them in motion in the sky through offering their own divine blood.

Aztec builders and stonemasons made reverent use of architectural and sculptural styles from these ancient cities in creating the sacred precinct of Tenochtitlán. Aztec

Above: In observatories such as the Caracol at Chichén Itzá, the patterns of the night sky were interpreted.

pilgrims took masks and other sacred items from graves in Teotihuacán and Tollán to reuse them in their own temple offerings in Tenochtitlán. Aztec priests and worshippers enthusiastically practised the rituals of human sacrifice which (although they had ancient beginnings in the Mesoamerican past) had been decisively escalated by the honoured Toltecs.

Below: Maya sculptors reached great heights of artistic expression. This head represents King Pacal of Palenque in middle age.

At Chichén Itzá in northern Yucatán, a group of Maya, also influenced by the Toltecs, similarly used *chacmools*, arranged the skulls of victims on skull racks and held vast public rites of human sacrifice.

DUALITY AND CHANGE

The Mesoamericans' understanding that time moved in cycles governed by the gods was balanced by an acute awareness of patterns of change and structures of duality. The Aztecs and the Maya understood the universe to be structured according to a divinely ordained duality: life and death, day and night, light and darkness, wet and dry, the celestial realm and the underworld realm all balanced one another. They also tended to succeed one another. Day was followed by night, the rainy season alternated with the dry season, life was followed by death – and then by new life. A king's death was the prelude to his voyage to the underworld, land of the dead, and followed by his ascent to the celestial realm. However, the gods could break this sacred pattern of alternation at any time.

Left: Sacred symbols in nature. This Maya vase from the Sula valley, Honduras, shows a divine monkey-spider and a bird-man.

Each night, the sun took the form of a jaguar and had to fight its way through the underworld during the hours of darkness before it could be reborn in the eastern sky. A day might come on which the gods withdrew their favour and the sun did not rise.

Within the complex patterns of years created by Mesoamericans' use of twin 260-day and 365-day calendars, the period of 52 solar years had great sacred significance. It measured the time that elapsed before a day in the 260-day calendar would coincide with a day in the 365-day calendar. The end of a 52-year cycle was also viewed as a time of particular danger, when the gods might be particularly inclined to break the patterns of succession and bring the world to an end. Priests ensured that the sacred calendars of ritual were observed with particular care at such times of risk.

FATE AND FATALISM

Across Mesoamerica, astronomer-priests made observations of the cycles of planets and movements of stars, while shaman-priests interpreted the ritual calendars and performed rites of divination using psychotrophic substances.

Those who relied on the statements of these experts believed that the diviners had the power to identify sacred influences on human activity in the

Above: Serpent imagery abounds in this Mixtec representation of water goddess Chalchiúhtlicue. The snake was associated with water, fertility and the earth.

patterns of the sky and in the cycles of time. Some historians argue that beliefs in divination, the power of omens and the inevitability of time's repeating patterns made Mesoamericans more fatalistic than they would otherwise have been when faced with a challenge.

The so-called 'Maya collapse' – when in the 9th and 10th centuries AD a series of powerful cities across Guatemala stopped erecting dated monuments to the glory of their kings and fell into rapid decline – had many causes, principally environmental degradation, but was possibly also encouraged by a fatalistic belief among some Maya that the decline could be predicted from the patterns of time, that, by the gods' choice, these events mirrored others many centuries earlier and so were not worth resisting.

Equally, there were many practical causes for the defeat of the mighty Aztec empire by a small band of Spanish invaders fighting in alliance with local peoples, but historical accounts reveal that Aztec leaders were aware that the omens were bad and appeared to prophesy their downfall. Some in Tenochtitlán thought Cortés was destined for victory, and some Aztecs even believed that Cortés was the Mesoamerican god Quetzalcóatl making a long-promised return to claim his rightful inheritance in Tenochtitlán.

DISCOVERING THE PAST

Mesoamericans themselves were Central America's first archaeologists. The Aztecs and Maya had a deep reverence for their own shared past and the achievements of their forebears, and investigated the evocative ruins of once majestic cities such as Tollán, Teotihuacán and Tikal.

Both Maya and Aztecs engaged with the ruined cities as religious centres rather than as historical sites. They came to satisfy a religious and cultural yearning to touch and be touched by the past. They saw nothing wrong in entering monuments and tombs to gather funerary masks and golden grave offerings for their own religious use, or in adding offerings of their own to a temple cache.

The Aztecs carried artefacts back from Teotihuacán and Tula to Tenochtitlán for use as temple offerings in the great Templo Mayor, where later generations of archaeologists would discover them. In Maya lands, pilgrims from Chichén Itzá may have travelled to the ruins of Tikal to perform religious ceremonies; in later times both Uxmal and Chichén Itzá were pilgrimage sites. The Aztecs also carried out sacrifices and sacred rites at the city of Teotihuacán.

The Spanish invaders of the early 16th century treated the great architectural achievements of Mesoamerica with scant respect. They set out to destroy the temples and religious statuary of the Aztecs, which they believed to be touched by evil. They erected the capital of their colony, New Spain, atop the rubble and shattered remnants of the Aztecs' great metropolis of Tenochtitlán.

Left: This view of the archway at Labná is by English artist Frederick Catherwood who, with American author John L. Stephens, was a pioneer of Maya exploration in the 1830s–40s. It is taken from their 1841 book on Maya ruins.

WONDERS IN THE JUNGLE

The first organized archaeological investigation of Mesoamerican ruins took place in the 17th century. A Mexican Jesuit priest called Carlos de Siguenza y Gongora (1645–1700) led a dig at Teotihuacán which mainly focused on the Pyramid of the Moon, as part of a lifelong attempt to research and write a history of ancient Mexico.

The 18th century saw the modern rediscovery of important Mesoamerican relics and sites, notably of Maya cities that had been abandoned and overgrown by tropical jungle. Palenque, in the densely forested foothills of the Chiapas mountains and overlooking the coastal plain that stretches 128km (80 miles) to the Gulf of Mexico, was rediscovered in 1746 by Padre Antonio Solis.

The first excavation of the Palenque site, which began in May 1786, was carried out by Spanish artillery captain Don Antonio del Río, who had orders from King Carlos III of Spain to search for gold and other valuables. Del Río left with a stucco head, the carved leg of a throne and other pieces of decorative carving, which he sent to Spain by way of Guatemala. Many years later, the captain's report of his excavations was published in English in London in 1822 with copies of del Río's sketches reproduced as lithographs by Johann-Friedrich Maximilien von Waldeck. The book generated interest in further investigation of Maya cities. It was followed by the publication in Paris in 1834 of *Antiquités Mexcaines*, the account of an 1805–6 visit to Palenque by Frenchman Guillaume Dupaix in the company of Mexican artist Luciano Castañeda. Waldeck himself visited the site in 1821 and published his own meticulously rendered images in 1865.

GODDESS IN THE EARTH
An important discovery had occurred at the site of the former Aztec capital Tenochtitlán in 1790. Workmen laying paving stones discovered a 2.5 metre (8ft)-tall stone statue of the Aztec earth

Above: Désiré Charnay, first to conduct archaeological excavations at Tula, made this engraving of Palenque in 1887.

goddess Coatlícue, together with a 3.6 metre (almost 12ft) diameter carved stone monument that commemorated the five suns or world ages of Aztec belief (later known as the Sun Stone). The finds were the first evidence of the wealth of archaeological remains that lay directly beneath the surface of Mexico City. The Sun Stone was placed on display on one of the towers of the city's Metropolitan Cathedral, while the statue of Coatlícue was given to the Royal and Pontifical University of Mexico.

THE TREASURES OF THE JUNGLE
In the 19th century, many of the great abandoned cities of the Maya civilization were rediscovered among dense jungle foliage and explored. An important catalyst for the surge of interest in central American ruins was the publication in 1841 of the two-volume *Incidents of Travel in Central America, Chiapas and Yucatán* by American traveller John Lloyd Stephens (1805–52). This work was based on an 1839–40 voyage to Honduras, Guatemala and Mexico, which was undertaken by Stephens in the

Left: This romanticized view of the Temple of the Cross, at Palenque, was made by Johann-Friedrich Maximilien von Waldeck.

company of English architect and artist Frederick Catherwood (1799–1854). Stephens and Catherwood visited the magnificent site of Copán, which Stephens was able to buy for $50, discovered Quiriguá and also examined Palenque and Uxmal. On a second voyage in 1841–2, the two men explored sites including Chichén Itzá, Cozumel, Tulum, Dzilam, Izamal and Ake. They published another two-volume survey, *Incidents of Travel in Yucatán*, in 1843. Sites they publicized include Copán, Palenque, Chichén Itzá, Tulum, Uxmal and Quiriguá.

TOWERS AMONG THE TREES

The remains of the great Classic Period Maya city of Tikal, in the northern part of the Petén region of Guatemala, were also rediscovered in the mid-19th century. They were first noticed by a local gum-sapper named Ambrosio Tut, who saw the roofcombs of the city's soaring pyramid temples while working at the top of a sapodilla tree.

Tut reported the finding to Modesto Méndez, Governor-Magistrate of the Petén region, and a six-day exploratory expedition was despatched by the Guatemalan government under Méndez and Tut in 1848. Méndez's report, with fanciful images by artist Eusebio Lara, was published that year in the Guatemalan newspaper *La Gaceta* and in 1853 in the magazine of the Berlin Academy of Sciences.

Significant later 19th-century expeditions to the site included that of the Swiss botanist Gustave Bernoulli, who removed carved sapodilla-wood lintels from Temples I and IV and carried them off to the Museum für Völkerkunde in Basel. They also included that of the English archaeologist-explorer Sir Alfred Percival Maudslay (1850–1931), who visited in 1881 and 1882. Using recently invented camera equipment, Sir Alfred took the earliest photographs of the city of Tikal's magnificent monuments.

Above: This Catherwood engraving, from the 1841 Incidents of Travel in Central America, Chiapas and Yucatán, *is of the partly overgrown Castillo in Chichén Itzá.*

Other cities were being rediscovered in the jungle. In 1882, Sir Alfred led an official Guatemalan government expedition to a major but little known settlement on the Usumacinta river. Then known as Macanche, the riverbank city was later renamed Yaxchilán.

With official approval, Sir Alfred removed the superbly carved lintels from Yaxchilán to prevent their loss to less scrupulous visitors. In the same year, the French explorer and archaeologist Désiré Charnay visited and photographed the site. At Copán, George Gordon of Harvard University's Peabody Museum led a three-year investigation in 1891–4.

In the 1880s, Désiré Charnay also conducted the first archaeological dig at the site identified as the capital of the Toltecs, near the modern town of Tula in Hidalgo State, Mexico. In 1873, Antonio García Cubas, a member of the Mexican Society of Geography and History, had published a written description of the site. Charnay went on to excavate two houses and the structure known as the Adoratorio, in the middle of the main square. Later archaeologists were less than impressed by his unsubtle methods. These

included the use of dynamite for clearance. Charnay did, however, also take some of the earliest photographs of ancient Mesoamerican ruins. He also experimented with papier-mâché to make impressions of ancient hieroglyphs.

Below: Beneath ground level in modern Mexico City archaeologists uncover Aztec remains. This is part of the Templo Mayor.

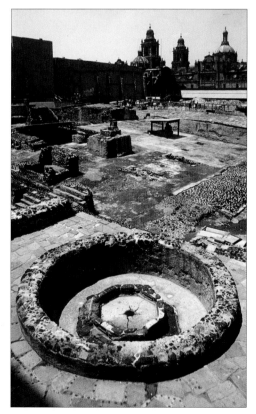

PAINSTAKING EXCAVATIONS

Throughout the 20th century, extensive and painstaking archaeological programmes gradually uncovered more and more evidence of how Mesoamericans lived, fought and worshipped.

CARNEGIE EXCAVATIONS

A pioneering archaeological project at Chichén Itzá in north-central Yucatán was led by Sylvanus Morley of the Carnegie Institution, Washington DC, for 20 years from 1924. The project excavated and restored many buildings, in the process discovering beneath them several almost intact constructions. These provided important evidence of the typical Mesoamerican building practice in which new structures were erected on top of their predecessors on sites already sanctified by ritual use. The work led to the scholarly division of Chichén Itzá's buildings into two groups. Those in the local 'Puuc style' from the end of the Classic Period and those exhibiting a Toltec-Mexican influence in the first years of the Postclassic Period.

The Carnegie Institution also conducted archaeological investigation at Uaxactún, 40km (25 miles) north of Tikal, in the years 1926–37. From the calendrical carvings, ceramic remains and buildings at Uaxactún, the Carnegie scholars plotted a chronology of cultural development for the region in the Classic Period that is still widely used by archaeologists today.

NEW MAP OF AN ANCIENT CITY

At Tikal, the combined efforts of Teobert Maler, Alfred Tozzer and R.E. Merwin led to the publication by Tozzer and Merwin of the first map of the site in 1911. Sylvanus Morley made a detailed study of Tikal's monuments and inscriptions on four visits in 1914, 1921, 1922 and 1928, while in 1926, Edwin Shook of the Carnegie Institution found a previously undiscovered group of buildings (now known as Group H) and two *sacbeob* or sacred causeways (now named in honour

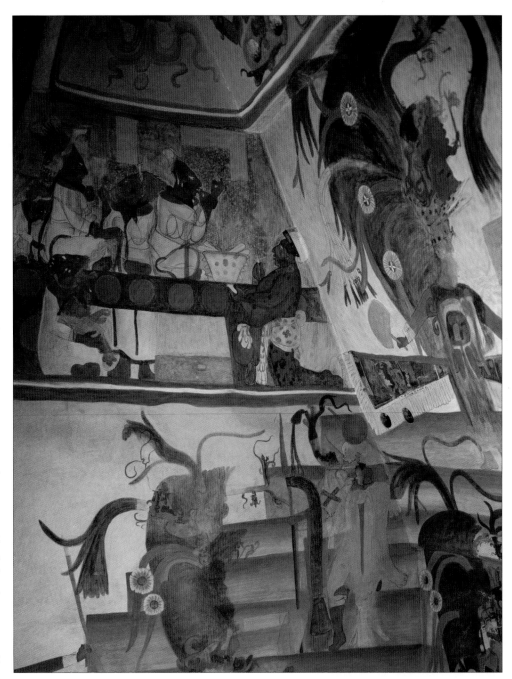

of Maudslay and Maler). Shook became the first field director of a major 14-year survey, the Tikal Project, which was conducted by the University Museum of Pennsylvania University 1956–70.

Major programmes were also carried out at Tula. In the 1930s, the work of ethnologist Wigberto Jimenez Moreno established that the site excavated by the Frenchman Désiré Charnay in the 19th

Above: A corner of one of the painted rooms at Bonampak depicts the members of the royal court enjoying a lavish feast.

century was the Toltecs' celebrated city, known also as Tollán. Subsequently, Jorge Acosta of the Mexican National Institute of Anthropology and History (INAH) led a 20-year archaeological programme at Tula in 1940–60, during which his teams investigated and partly restored one of the site's ball courts (now known as Ball Court 1), Temples B and C, the Coatepantli and the Palacio de Quetzalcóatl. Based on pottery remains, Acosta also worked out a chronology of events and occupying groups for the site. His work was extended through joint excavations by the University of Missouri Colombia (UMC) under Richard Diehl and an INAH team under Eduardo Matos Moctezuma in 1966–76.

The second INAH team conducted a major survey of the surrounding land and restored a second ball court. Together with that of the UMC, their work established that Tula was a large and lively city, at its peak and that, for a period, it was Mesoamerica's prime power.

PAINTED WALLS
About 30km (18 miles) to the south of Yaxchilán, in the densely forested valley of the Río Lacanha in Chiapas state, a Maya site previously known only to locals was revealed to the wider world in 1946. American photographer Giles Healey was on a field trip looking for picturesque ruins when his guides led him to a small settlement they called Bonampak ('Painted Walls'). Healey found a three-roomed building containing vivid, brightly coloured images of court life in a Maya

Above: The ball court at Palenque lies to the north-east of the imposing Palace and the celebrated Temple of Inscriptions.

city during the 8th century AD. His report and pictures naturally provoked wide interest and the Carnegie Institute organized an archaeological programme at the site, which also contains an acropolis, a large plaza and a number of stelae. As at some other major Maya sites such as Palenque, there are buildings still unexcavated in the surrounding forest.

PALENQUE'S STEPPED PYRAMID
At Palenque, Sylvanus Morley, Oliver LaFarge, Franz Blom and Edward Seler all carried out work in the early part of the 20th century. In 1952, Mexican architect Alberto Ruz Lhuillier discovered the magnificent royal tomb of King Pacal, Palenque's ruler in the 7th–8th

centuries AD, in a crypt beneath the Temple of Inscriptions. Historians had believed that Maya stepped pyramids were used only as temple platforms; that is, to lift their temples above other buildings; Lhuiller's find was the first indication that the pyramids were in some places built primarily as royal funerary monuments.

TENOCHTITLÁN
In the centre of what was once Tenochtitlán, a major excavation of the Aztecs' great temple, the Templo Mayor, began in 1978. The programme was inspired by a chance find, when an electrical company worker digging in central Mexico City uncovered part of a clearly remarkable sculpture. The team of archaeologists who took over to clear away debris uncovered a vast monolith, 3.25m (10ft) in diameter, representing the dismembered form of the goddess Coyolxauhqui who, in Aztec creation narrative, was cut up by her brother Huitzilopochtli in the first moments of his life.

Excavation revealed that the Aztecs built the Templo Mayor in layers, each new construction enclosing an earlier structure. Archaeologists uncovered the successive constructions back to *c.*1390, showing the twin shrines to rain god Tláloc and Lord Huitzilopochtli.

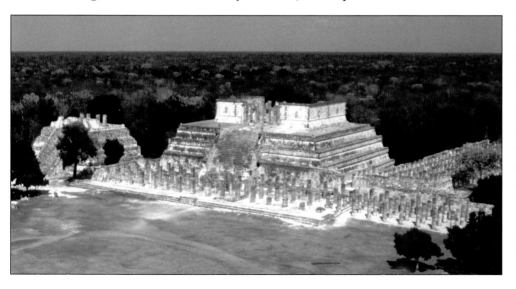

Left: The Group of the Thousand Columns is one of the imposing structures in Chichén Itzá reflecting later, Toltec, influence.

TRANSLATING AN ANCIENT WRITING

The first modern visitors to Maya sites such as Yaxchilán or Copán were enthralled by tall stelae elegantly carved with inscriptions in artistically arranged picture glyphs. Historians were also deeply intrigued by the writing in four surviving Maya codices and by a list of glyphs presented as the 'Maya alphabet' by Bishop Diego de Landa in his 16th-century work, *Relacion de las Cosas de Yucatán*. Historians were frustrated that they could not read this ancient writing and so glean invaluable information about the Maya way of life.

DECIPHERING THE PAST

In the years up to the 1950s, linguists made slow but steady progress in interpreting Maya writing. Figures such as Léon de Rosny, Ernst Förstemann, Sylvanus Morley and J. Eric Thompson catalogued the glyphs and successfully identified some. Förstemann and Rosny, for example, translated the glyphs for 'north', 'south', 'east', 'west', 'zero' and 'twenty'. However, the entire world of Maya scholarship laboured under two misconceptions. The scholars wrongly believed that the inscriptions on Maya stelae contained religious and astronomical information, but no historical facts. Historians were also mistaken in their belief that the glyphs were logographic. The pictures represented whole words or ideas and did not stand for spoken sounds.

The first misconception was removed by the work of Heinrich Berlin and Tatiana Proskouriakoff in the 1950s. Berlin, a German-Mexican scholar, first identified an emblem glyph specific to each of several Maya sites and suggested that it recorded the place name or the name of the ruling dynasty. Proskouriakoff, a Russian-American expert on Maya art, then showed that carved inscriptions on stelae at Piedras Negras celebrated the birth, accession to the throne and other life events of a series of rulers of that city. In her work on Piedras Negras and then Yaxchilán, she identified glyphs for 'was born', 'acceded to throne', 'captor', 'captured' and 'died'.

Above: Stela 6 from Piedras Negras shows the king seated cross-legged in a recess with glyphs dating the monument to AD687.

The second misconception was laid to rest, also in the 1950s, by the Soviet linguist Yuri V. Knorosov, who demonstrated that, alongside their function as logograms, the glyphs had a 'phonetic' element; they represented spoken sounds. Working with the de Landa 'alphabet', Knorosov saw that many of the elements of the list were not letters but syllables combining a consonant and a vowel. There were no signs for a single consonant. When writing a word with the pattern consonant-vowel-consonant, he argued, a Maya scribe would use two of the combined signs, consonant-vowel plus consonant-vowel. The vowel in the second sign would match that in the first, but would be read as silent. For example, to write the word *cutz* ('turkey'), a scribe

Left: 'Emblem glyphs' specific to particular cities were identified by Heinrich Berlin in 1958. The symbols identifying the cities were written with a pair of affixes (appended signs) meaning 'holy king of'.

emblem-glyph affixes

a bat
(Copán)

a cacao tree with
pod (Quiriguá)

'cleft sky'
(Yaxchilán)

a bundle
(Tikal)

'Quincunx'
(Piedras Negras)

a bone
(Palenque)

a skull
(Palenque)

Cauac
(Seibal)

crossed sky
bands (Naranjo)

bundle
(Petexbatun)

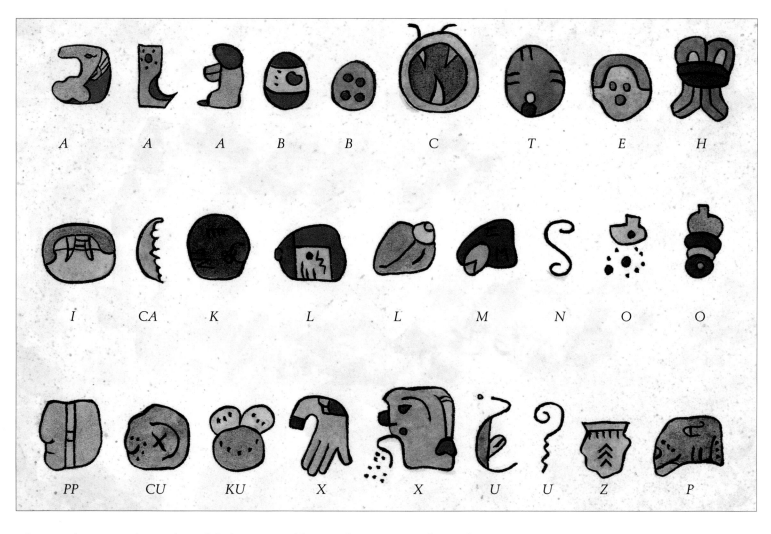

| A | A | A | B | B | C | T | E | H |

| I | CA | K | L | L | M | N | O | O |

| PP | CU | KU | X | X | U | U | Z | P |

Above: Bishop Diego de Landa's 'alphabet' of Maya writing was dismissed by scholars until linguist Yuri Knorosov showed that it was a list of syllables rather than an 'abc'.

Left: In a detail from Piedras Negras Stela 40, an individual performs a sacred rite of scattering in honour of an ancestor.

would write the signs *cu* and *tzu*. The two *Us* would agree, and the word would be read 'cutz' (with the last u silent.) The idea that the vowels would agree was dubbed 'synharmony' by Knorosov.

Knorosov's theory provoked outrage among many Maya scholars, but has proved to be largely correct. As Knorosov argued, Maya script contains both logographs and phonetic elements. The latest thinking is that the script, which was in use for more than 1,500 years, was originally mainly logosyllabic (pictures stood for syllables or words), but over time increasingly included more phonetic elements. However, further progress in deciphering Maya script has partially undermined Knorosov's idea of synharmony. When words were spelled phonetically, they often did not have the matching vowels that his theory suggested they should.

REINTERPRETATIONS

Historians have continued to make breakthroughs in interpreting glyphs, often with important implications for our understanding of the Maya. In 1979, Peter Matthews showed that an ear spool found at Altun Ha in Belize was labelled *u tup* ('his ear spool') with the name of the owner. Several other writers have since shown that the practice Matthews termed 'name tagging' was used by the Maya on bowls, plates and carved bones.

David Stuart and Stephen Houston have identified a glyph used to describe the spirit familiar or companion that Mesoamericans believed accompanied each of us. The discovery has led to the reinterpetation of many scenes on Maya pots or stelae, where figures once thought to be gods or rulers can now be positively identified as spirit familiars.

Linguistic work has also revealed that the Maya referred to stelae as 'stone trees' and to the objects historians generally label 'altars' as 'stone thrones'.

17

PART ONE

THE MESOAMERICAN WORLD

In a time before time, Huitzilopochtli, tribal god of the México/Aztecs, sprang from his mother fully armed to defend her against his jealous siblings on the sacred heights of Mount Coatepetl. In the mature years of the fifth sun or world age of the Aztecs, in the ceremonial precinct of the imperial capital Tenochtitlán, the great mass of the Templo Mayor was celebrated as a recreation of the mountain where the tribal god was born and was called Coatepetl or Coatepec. Both Aztec and Maya architects intended their temple-platforms to represent sacred mountains as part of a wider desire to honour and recreate in their cities and social organization the holy patterns of the natural world.

Mesoamericans saw divine meaning threaded through all natural phenomena. Theirs was a sacred universe, whose rules were established in the 'holy time' of religious narrative. They performed sacrificial ritual in obedience to demands established in this holy time, as a way of honouring the creative sacrifice of the gods.

This survey of the Mesoamerican world begins with a look at its terrains and wildlife, then examines the spread of human settlement across Middle America. It then proceeds to describe the vibrant trade that fuelled much of this expansion and to investigate Mesoamerican patterns of daily life and work, before concluding with a description of the ways in which Mesoamericans celebrated the sacred patterns of their universe in religious life and culture.

Maya warriors attack a village in Yucatán. As among the Aztecs, successful warriors were rewarded with social prestige and preferential treatment in the afterlife.

TIMELINE OF MESOAMERICA

PRECLASSIC PERIOD TO AD250

Above: Olmec stone heads may have been used in rites honouring royal ancestors.

3114BC The start date of the Maya Long Count dating system is equivalent to 13 August 3114BC.

2300BC Artist at Tlapacoya makes the oldest surviving ceramic figurine.

1400BC Oldest known ball court constructed at Paso de la Amada, Chiapas.

c.1400BC Potters in highland Mexico, fashion many ceramic figurines, probably for use as grave offerings.

1250–900BC Olmecs lay out pyramids and courts in their holy town of San Lorenzo.

1200BC Coapexco becomes a centre for the growing trade in obsidian.

1100BC Olmec influence seen in rock carvings at the trading centre of Chalcatzingo.

800–500BC Olmec stone heads set up in La Venta. Maya settlers build the pyramid Mound 30a at Izapa.

500BC The Zapotec city of Monte Albán is established in Oaxaca.

300BC Zapotec builders construct the main plaza of Monte Albán.

250BC Building of the North Acropolis begins at Tikal.

c.200BC Carvings of war prisoners added to Building L at Monte Albán.

200BC–AD300 Building J, an astronomical observatory and military conquest monument built at Monte Albán.

150BC–AD150 Vast El Tigre monument built in the Maya city of El Mirador.

100BC–AD150 Teotihuacán established as a sacred city and a major population centre. The Pyramid of the Sun is built and the Street of the Dead laid out.

31BC Stela C at Trez Zapotes, on the Mexican Gulf Coast, is carved with a date in the Maya Long Count equivalent to 3 September 31BC.

AD36 Stela 1 at El Baúl, Guatemala, is carved with a standing figure and the date AD36.

AD100 A ball court is built at Monte Albán.

AD156 Stela 1 at La Mojarra in Veracruz is carved with a standing figure and the dates AD143 and AD156.

c.AD200 The *talud-tablero* architectural feature is used on the Temple of the Feathered Serpent in Teotihuacán's Citadel area.

c.AD250 Artists decorate Teotihuacán temples with wall paintings.

C.AD250–900 CLASSIC PERIOD

Above: Tikal was a major city by AD300 and at its zenith in the 8th century AD.

AD300 The Zapotecs of Monte Albán establish the nearby settlement of Mitla, which contains many tombs. They call it Lyobaa ('Site of Burials').

AD400 Teotihuacáno influence is seen at the Maya site of Kaminaljuyú, where buildings begin to use the *talud-tablero* architectural feature.

AD426 The first ritual buildings are erected at Copán in the reign of King Yax Kuk Mo' (*r.* AD426–37).

AD647 King Pacal (*r.* AD615–83) begins a major building programme at the city of Palenque, with the construction of the Olvidado temple ('Unnoticed Shrine') to the west of the main plaza.

AD650 Potters at Remojadas and other sites in Veracruz produce ceramic figures for use in religious ritual.

AD692 At Palenque the temples of the Cross Group are dedicated.

c.AD700 El Tajín, in Veracruz, contains 12 ball courts and the remarkable Pyramid of the Niches, which contains 365 openings, one for each day of the solar year.

C.AD250–900 CLASSIC PERIOD

AD726 In Yaxchilán Lord Shield Jaguar (*r.* AD681–742) dedicates Temple 23 (Queen's House) to his wife, Lady Xoc.

AD734 Tikal's King Ah Cacau (*r.* AD682–734) buried beneath Temple I, which he built as his funerary monument.

AD738 King 18-Rabbit (*r.* AD695–78) completes building work on the Great Ball Court at Copán.

AD749 Copán's King Smoke Shell (*r.* AD749–763) completes the Hieroglyphic Stairway.

*c.*AD750 Builders erect Tikal's Temple VI (Temple of the Inscriptions) and the city's tallest building, Temple IV – 70m (230ft) tall.

*c.*AD750 Artists at Cacaxtla paint a series of magnificent murals.

AD775 At Copán, King Yax Pac (*r.* AD763–820) dedicates the monument known as Altar Q, which bears portraits of all 16 kings of the dynasty founded by Yax Kuk Mo'.

*c.*AD800 Tula/Tollán is laid out, like Teotihuacán, on a grid pattern.

*c.*AD900 Builders at Chichén Itzá erect the Caracol, perhaps as a temple to the wind god, but more likely as an astronomical observatory.

*c.*AD900 The Pyramid of the Feathered Serpent is built at Xochicalco.

POSTCLASSIC AND MODERN PERIODS AD900–2005

AD909 Monument 101 at Toniná is last carving with date in the Maya Long Count.

*c.*1230 The *Grolier Codex*, a calendar of the cycles of the planet Venus, is written.

*c.*1325 The México/Aztecs build the Templo Mayor in Tenochtitlán.

*c.*1345 The *Dresden Codex* is made.

*c.*1390 A larger pyramid-temple is constructed over the original Templo Mayor.

1431 The México/Aztecs build a third and much larger version of the Templo Mayor on the same site in Tenochtitlán.

1450–1500 A series of fine murals are painted in the Maya city of Tulum.

*c.*1450 The *Paris Codex* is compiled, perhaps in the Maya city of Mayapán.

1469 México/Aztec artisans carve a stone image of Coyolxauhqui to place at the foot of a staircase on the western face of the Templo Mayor pyramid.

22 Aug 1700 Death of Carlos de Siguenza y Gongora, Jesuit priest, pioneering historian and the first to lead archaeological investigations at Teotihuacán.

1746 Ruins of Palenque discovered.

May 1786 First archaeological investigations at Palenque.

1840 John Lloyd Stephens finds Quiriguá.

1848 First expedition to explore Tikal.

1853 Report on Tikal by Modesto Méndez published by Berlin Academy of Science.

Above: The first archaeological investigations at Palenque were in 1786.

1882 Sir Alfred Maudslay leads an official exploration of Yaxchilán.

1924–44 The Carnegie Institution (Washington DC) carries out an archaeological programme at Chichén Itzá.

1940–60 Acosta leads dig at Tula/Tollán.

1946 Giles Healey discovers Bonampak.

1971 Ancient sacred cave found beneath Pyramid of the Sun, Teotihuacán.

1978 Electrical worker discovers vast carving of Coyolxauhqui in Mexico City.

1997 'Codex' murals found at Mayapán.

1998 Archaeologists discover the oldest known Mesoamerican ball court at Paso de la Amada, Chiapas, *c.*1400BC.

2002 Guatemalan Maya jade artefacts found in an elite ceremonial burial at Teotihuacán's Pyramid of the Moon.

2003 Finds at San Andrés suggest the Olmec used a logographic writing system.

CHAPTER ONE

LAND OF DANGER AND REWARD

The Aztecs and Maya made their home in an unstable and unpredictable physical environment. They feared the sudden shiftings of the 'earth monster' when earthquakes struck. They dreaded the onset of drought, the tightening of the dry earth that squeezes life out of the withering crops. They were wary of the beasts of jungle and plain, not least the majestic jaguar; in coastal regions they fled the onslaught of hurricanes and violent storms.

They saw the gods and goddesses everywhere. Partly because the world could turn on them suddenly and destructively, they became convinced of the need to honour the gods. The Aztecs, following long-established Mesoamerican practice, believed that the cycle of the sun's morning birth following death at evening might suddenly stop if blood sacrifices to the gods were not maintained. Equally, Mesoamericans celebrated the gods for the glory of divine energy and the pattern of sacred meaning they saw in all things.

Life in Mesoamerica, lived in the presence of death and catastrophe, was keenly experienced. Mesoamericans entered an intense relationship with their land, a region of rich contrasts – from the mountains of highland Mexico to the plains of the Pacific and Gulf Coasts, from desert and semi-arid landscapes to river valleys, lake shores and the dense jungles of lowland Guatemala.

Left: Aztecs and Maya feared the anger of the region's many volcanoes. The oval crater of Popocatépetl has near-vertical sides. Poisonous volcanic gases erupt from vents in the walls.

HIGHLAND AND LOWLAND

Mesoamerica's first settlers in the second millennium BC could choose between living at sea level along estuaries rich in marine life, in well-watered lowland tropical forests teeming with animals or on dry, elevated plateaux surrounded by rocky uplands well provided with minerals and other resources. Their choice of altitude would largely have determined the climate they would have experienced.

ALTITUDE VARIATIONS

From sea level up to altitudes of about 900m (3,000ft), in lands dubbed *tierra caliente* ('hot territory'), average temperatures were high, with little seasonal variation. In these low-lying tropical regions today, the temperature variation between summer and winter months is generally as little as 5°C and winter is marked by the coming of the rains. In Veracruz, the region on the Gulf of Mexico where the Olmec civilization emerged in the second millennium BC,

Below: Pine forests occupy elevated tierra fria *('cold territory') beneath the peak of Nevado de Toluca, 4,577m (15,016ft) high.*

the average year-round daily temperature is 25°C (77°F). Average temperatures of 24–28°C (75–82°F) hold in the Yucatán peninsula, which was home to many northern Maya settlements.

At altitudes of 900–1,800m (3,000–6,000ft), in *tierra templada* ('temperate territory'), average temperatures are about 5°C lower. The mountaintop Zapotec city of Monte Albán sat at an altitude of 1,600m (5,200ft); average temperatures in the region today are around 18°C (64°F). At 1,800–3,400m (6,000–11,000ft) or *tierra fria* ('cold territory') an average temperature is 5°C or lower, with much greater seasonal variation than at higher altitude. Mexico City, which arose on the ruins of Aztec Tenochtitlán, lies at 2,300m (7,500ft) and has an average daily temperature of 15°C (59°F). Temperatures there can rise to 26°C (78°F) in the hottest month (May) and may fall to a low of 12°C (54°F) in the coldest month (January).

With experience, Mesoamericans discovered that the deep-coloured highland soils of the Valley of Mexico or the Valley of Oaxaca were extremely

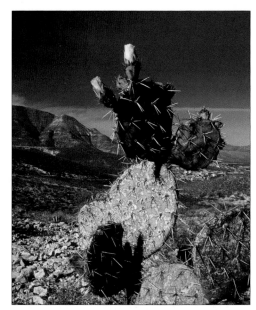

Above: Parched highlands such as this sweep of desert north of Chihuahua, Mexico, are typically rich in minerals.

mineral-rich and could be farmed intensively and on steep slopes. By comparison the earth in such lowland areas as El Petén in Guatemala often needed to be left fallow for prolonged periods to safeguard its fertility. Here farmers developed slash-and-burn agriculture, in which land was cleared with fire then used for perhaps three seasons before being left for as many as ten to recover its richness.

RAINFALL VARIATION

In parts of Mesoamerica drought was a persistent threat. Today, the Valley of Mexico receives as little as 600mm (23in) of rain in a year. However, other regions receive such abundant precipitation that they can support the vibrant growth of tropical rainforests. The Gulf coastal plain as far east as Tabasco, adjoining the Chiapas highlands, in whose foothills the great Maya city of Palenque arose, generally receives an annual average of 2,000mm (78in) of rain. To the southeast, in the jungle region of El Petén, average rainfall is around 1,350mm (53in) each year.

Above: Swamplands on the Mexican Gulf Coast made a resource-rich home for the earliest Mesoamerican settlers.

DROUGHTS OF THE 1450s

In the first years of rule by the Aztec *tlatoani* Moctezuma I (1440–69), a series of terrible calamities befell the peoples of the Valley of Mexico. In 1446 their harvests were lost to a plague of locusts, then in 1449 the island city of Tenochtitlán was flooded. Frosts and drought struck the crops for four consecutive years in 1450–4.

Chronicle accounts suggest that at the close of the 16th century – 150 years afterwards – people still told breathless tales of the privations of these times, when the weak and starving went hopelessly in search of food and watched with despairing eyes the circling shadows of vultures on the bone-dry ground. Sacrifices were urgently offered to the gods and finally, in 1455, the goggle-eyed rain god Tláloc returned with drenching rains. The people rejoiced in a bumper harvest of maize.

Across Mesoamerica the rainy season generally occurs between June and October. Rainfall can be very strong at the height of the season. Mexico City typically receives almost one third of its annual rainfall of 160mm (6in) in July alone, while Tabasco may be hit by 300mm (11in) in its wettest month (September). In El Petén the rainy season runs from June to December.

FLOODS AND HURRICANES

The Mesoamerican region was also vulnerable to storms, hurricanes and flooding. The Aztecs in their island city of Tenochtitlán were subject to periodic flooding, when the waters of Lake Texcoco rose with the spring rains. The east coast of Mexico adjoining the Gulf of Mexico and the eastern edge of the Yucatán peninsula frequently lay in the path of hurricanes. The Aztec god Tezcatlipoca had special power over hurricane winds, as did the Palenque god Tahil (Obsidian Mirror) and the Quiché Maya sky god Huracán.

The land was young: the great peaks of Citlaltépetl and Popocatépetl were recent outcrops in geological terms, having been driven upwards in the late Tertiary period (as little as 1.6 million years ago).

Mesoamericans must have felt deep respect for the untameable power of nature. They lived in one of the most dynamic areas of the Earth for volcanic and seismic activity and were familiar with the shudderings of the earth monster and the periodic explosions of the volcanoes that spotted the landscape.

Below: Tezcatlipoca, Lord of the Hurricane, was feared for his capricious nature. The Aztecs called him called Yáotl ('Adversary').

25

TOWERING TREES, ROCKY SANDS

Many Maya made their living among dense jungle forests, tracking game or the rare quetzal bird, cutting back and burning the dense growth to fashion fields to grow crops and raising great stone temples that rivalled the height of the towering jungle trees. The wide variety of terrains, altitudes and climates encompassed by the Maya territories produced a range of distinct forests.

In the Alta Verapaz of Guatemala, at the northern edge of the southern Maya highlands, stand the highland rainforests, home of the rare and sacred quetzal, whose brightly coloured tail feathers were a valued item of trade among the Maya and other Mesoamericans. These humid

Below: The partly ruined Nohuch Mul pyramid rises 24m (80ft) to imitate a natural mountain at the Maya city of Cobá.

greenlands, sometimes called cloud forests, are dense with tropical growth of evergreens, lichens and mosses, delicate wild orchids, bromeliads and astonishing ferns that reach a height of 15m (50ft). Here professional hunters would track the quetzal in order to capture it alive, pluck its wondrous tail feathers and then set it free once more. In the wild the bird would grow new feathers after moulting.

STOREYED FOREST LIFE

In the lower altitude and denser rainforests of the southern Maya lowlands, different types of plant life thrive at distinct levels above ground. At the topmost level, perhaps 70m (230ft) above ground, towering mahogany and ceiba, a form of cottonwood, predominate. At a lower level, up to 50m (165ft) above ground, Spanish cedar, sapodilla, bari and

Above: The Lacandón rainforest in Chiapas, an ancient Maya homeland, is today under threat from farmers and loggers.

American fig trees grow densely. A third level, at up to 25m (80ft) in height, is vibrant with palms, avocado trees, rubber trees, breadnut trees and others. Vines, bromeliads and lianas climb their trunks. Beneath, at ground level, in dense shade, young trees and ferns are found.

TREE OF LIFE

The majestic ceiba, or silk-cotton tree, was sacred to the Maya and identified by them as the cosmic tree or tree of life. They believed that it linked the levels of the universe, sinking its roots through the earth to the lowest of the nine levels of the underworld and sending its towering branches to the topmost of the 13 levels of heaven. In some versions of their cosmology, the Maya told that five great trees supported the heavens, one in each of the four points of the compass and a fifth, the green ceiba, in the centre.

The vines that hang far down from the great ceiba's branches may have symbolized a spirit voyage from the ground level of earthly reality to the heights of heaven in the tree's great umbrella-shaped canopy. There, far above the forest floor, both epiphytes (aerial plants) and many species of animal make their home;

10m (30ft), palms, allspice and other species predominate. The growth of ferns and young trees at ground level is less vibrant here than further south. Here and there the forest gives way to seasonal swamps and grasslands. Tikal, Uaxactún, El Mirador and Calakmul all arose to glory in the central lowlands.

A PLACE OF NO CULTURE

At the other extreme of Mesoamerican terrains lay arid or semi-arid regions such as the wide plateau where the Toltec capital of Tollán was founded in highland Mexico and regions in Guatemala such as the Motagua Valley in the Maya highlands. In such areas the cult of the rain god was prominent and knowledge of irrigation techniques was key to agricultural success. Desert lay to the north in the northern part of the Mexican plateau, a region characterized by the Aztecs and their fellow inhabitants of the Valley of Mexico as a place of no culture, the place from which they had escaped in moving south. In the *Historia Tolteca Chichimeca*, an image of the seven caves from which the tribes were said to have emerged depicts several types of cacti, indicating that the primal landscape of origin in the first days was a sunblasted desert.

Above: Dry lands. Hunters cross a stretch of desert in a detail from the Mapa Tlotzin, *a genealogy of the governors of Texcoco.*

Below: At Labná in Yucatán, trees crowd close to the palace arch. To either side are stone representations of Maya village huts.

birds nest, mammals move about along the great branches, even frogs raise their young in the pools that form on branches and in tree trunks.

The ceiba blooms in the evening, producing tiny flowers very reminiscent of the ear flares worn by kings in Maya carving and ceramic images. Some authorities suggest that the king dressed himself as the silk-cotton tree, to signify that he was blessed like the holy ceiba and that he anchored the kingdom in sacred order. The carving on the lid of the sarcophagus in which King Pacal of Palenque was interred shows the king descending into the spirit realm of the underworld along the length of the cosmic tree. The Maya carved great canoes from the vast trunk of their sacred tree.

SEASONAL RAINFOREST

Farther north, in the region known as the central lowlands, the jungle is described as 'seasonal rainforest' because each year extended dry periods interrupt the supply of rainwater. The upper canopy of American fig, ceiba and mahogany is lower and often less complete, but still climbs to 50m (165ft) above ground. Beneath, a thick growth of fig, sapodilla and other trees form a very dense canopy, while lower still, at a height of around

LIFE IN THE WILD

The lands of the Aztecs and Maya were teeming with animal life. Mesoamericans so revered these creatures for their energy and marvellous abilities that they cast many of them in religious and creation narratives and even saw some, such as the jaguar and eagle, as principal physical forms of great gods.

KING JAGUAR

Throughout the region, the jaguar was king. The largest member of the *felidae* family of cats, the jaguar (*Felis onca*) can thrive in scrubland and desert as well as in its preferred habitat of dense forests and swamps. It can climb with ease and track prey along branches tens of metres above ground, but is also happy to leap into water and is a strong swimmer. The male, which is significantly larger than the female, can grow to 2.7m (9ft) in length and weigh up to 160kg (350lbs.) The jaguar hunts alone. It prefers to stalk

Below: Bird sacred to Huitzilopochtli. This detail of a stone carving on the Platform of the Jaguars and Eagles at Chichén Itzá depicts an eagle eating a human heart.

peccaries (pig-like mammals) and the capybara (a large rodent), but will also kill and eat deer, sloths, monkeys, anteaters, alligators, birds, turtles and even fish. The jaguar does not usually attack humans, unless cornered, when it is a savage opponent.

The jaguar played an important role in Mesoamerican religious life from early times. In the second millennium BC, Olmec craftsmen were carving intriguing jaguar-faced figures resembling human babies. The jaguar was associated with the ancient practice of shamanism (spirit travel) and was adopted by shamans as one of their animal forms.

Because of its fearsome capacity to hunt in darkness, it was an animal aspect of Tezcatlipoca, the Aztec lord of night and of dark fate, while elsewhere in Mesoamerica it was associated with the god of the underworld and with the realm of darkness. When the sun visited the underworld by night, it took the form of the jaguar. Like the lion in Europe, the jaguar became a symbol of royalty and bravery in Mesoamerica: Maya kings wore its pelt and were named after the jaguar, while in the Aztec army the two elite groups of fighters were called eagle and jaguar warriors.

The Aztecs called the jaguar *océlotl*. The smaller cat now known as the ocelot was known to the Aztecs as the *tlacaoocélotl* (literally, 'little jaguar'; *Felis pardalis*).

HUNTING ANIMALS AND BIRDS

When Mesoamericans went hunting they most commonly killed rabbits and white-tailed deer. Rabbits, perhaps because of their skittering speed of movement and rapid rate of reproduction, were associated by the Aztecs with drunkenness and with the alcoholic drink *pulque*. Maya and Aztec people also killed and ate ducks, geese, swans and other birds. The Hero Twins of Mayan mythology were celebrated for their skill in hunting birds using blowpipes.

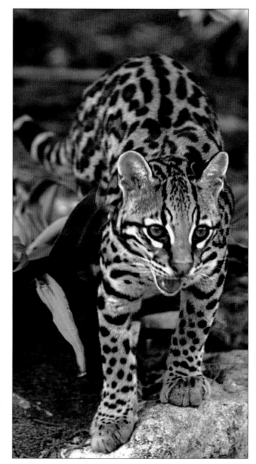

Above: Ocelots, known to the Aztecs as 'little jaguars', were common in the fertile lowlands of Mesoamerica along with opossums and tapirs.

Mesoamericans also hunted the rare quetzal bird, which was tracked and captured for its magnificent tail plumes, but never killed. The quetzal is found in the highland cloud forests that run from Chiapas to western Panama. Just 35cm (14in) long, it has tail feathers of up to 1m (3ft 3in) in length. These plumes change colour in the light, a shimmer of gold, emerald green and blue that sets off the bird's bright red breast.

Only the male bird possesses the iridescent tail feathers that are so highly prized: as with the peacock and peahen, the female bird is much plainer in appearance. The quetzal was an animal form of the great Plumed Serpent

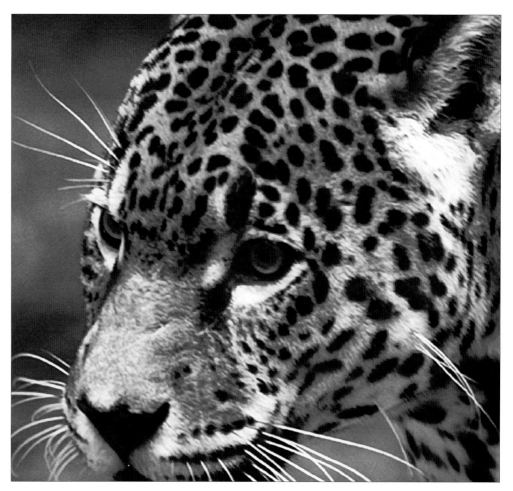

Quetzalcóatl and the feathers of the sacred bird were, like the jaguar pelt, symbolic of kingly authority.

Probably the most revered of birds was the eagle. An animal form taken by the Aztecs' tribal god Huitzilopochtli, it was central to Aztec origin narrative: the México/Aztecs founded their city of Tenochtitlán at the place where they saw an eagle destroying a snake upon a cactus, in fulfilment of a prophecy of Huitzilopochtli. The harpy eagle was found in the jungles of Maya lands while the golden eagle was known in central Mexico.

Other notable birds included parrots, macaws and toucans, falcons, owls, hawks and other birds of prey and, in estuaries and along coastlines, herons, giant storks and egrets. In the *Popol Vuh* of the Quiché Maya, the scarlet macaw, a vividly coloured species of parrot, attempted to set himself up as the pre-eminent god and to take the place of the sun, but he was outwitted by the Hero Twins. The hummingbird was another bird associated with Huitzilopochtli by the Aztecs.

BATS

The bat was also widely found. In the jungle bats nested beneath the vast roots of the ceiba that was viewed as the tree of life and understood to link the earth with the underworld and the heavens. Partly for this reason, and partly because of their natural associations with darkness, bats were linked to the underworld. The Zapotecs of Monte Albán associated the bat god with maize and fertility.

SNAKES AND MONKEYS

The snake was a complex and central religious symbol, associated with Tláloc and the rain, with the fertility of the earth, with the sun and heavens, with sacrificial blood and with religious and visionary experience. Mesoamericans also revered turtles and crocodiles: they sometimes said that the earth took the form of a crocodile or was resting on the back of a giant turtle. The Maya also identified the constellation Orion as a celestial turtle.

Monkeys were common in the lowlands. Species included howlers, spider monkeys and marmosets. Howlers, stocky, bearded monkeys up to 70cm (28in) long, live mainly in the upper branches of trees and would rarely have been seen. However, they would certainly have been heard: they take their name from the extremely resonant howl that they emit at dawn and dusk and during storms. The howler's cry can be heard more than 5km (as much as 3 miles) away. Marmosets are small, long-tailed monkeys that move quickly along branches, while spider monkeys are much larger with pot bellies. They forage in small groups among the very highest jungle branches. They rarely descend to the ground, but can be seen leaping from one tree to another. The Quiché Maya creators of the *Popul Vuh* narrative, which imagines a series of failed creations before the current one, told that monkeys were the descendants of a failed race of wooden people fashioned in early days by the creators.

Above: The jaguar is the largest New World cat. Like the lion in Europe, it became a symbol of royalty and bravery in Mexico.

Below: The intricate decoration in the Nunnery Quadrangle, Uxmal, contains twin images of the sacred rattlesnake.

FRUITS OF THE EARTH

The first humans in Mesoamerica were hunter-gatherers who survived on a diet of seeds and plants supplemented both by mammoths and mastodons and by smaller game, birds and fish. They lived in this way for many millennia before beginning to domesticate plants such as avocados, squash, beans and chilli peppers and turning to a settled, agricultural way of life.

PEOPLE OF MAIZE

The plant that would become their descendants' staple food – maize – was probably first domesticated from a wild cereal grass called *teosinte*. Archaeological evidence from the Tehuacán Valley in the Puebla region to the south-east of the Valley of Mexico suggests that, in the wild, the grass produced cobs that were no more than 2.5cm (1in) long: at this size, they could be an addition to a diet but not a staple food. In domesticating the plant, the first Mesoamerican farmers

Below: Images of the revered maize plant were carved on the sides of this basalt block used as an altar by the Aztecs.

succeeded in enlarging the cobs. In the wild, beans and squash grew alongside *teosinte* and other grasses, climbing up the grass stalks in the protection of the shade provided by the leaves. The first farmers, who had already domesticated varieties of squash and beans, might have copied this method of planting.

Archaeologists report that the first cereal domesticated in Mesoamerica was not *teosinte* but another, related to modern grain millet (*Setaria geniculata*). *Teosinte* itself was probably first domesticated in the lands adjoining the Balsas river of western Mexico some centuries before 5000BC. From archaeological remains we know that its use spread slowly eastwards, reaching the Tehuacán Valley by *c*.5000BC, Oaxaca by *c*.4000BC and Veracruz by *c*.2250BC. Its first cultivators perfected the making of stone mortars and used them to grind the maize ears.

Mesoamericans saw themselves as people reliant on, dedicated to and even made of maize. The word used by the Aztecs for the maize dough from which

Above: Xilonen, the Aztec goddess of young maize cobs, was worshipped in the form of a virginal adolescent girl.

they made tortillas is *toneuhcayotl* ('our flesh'). In some versions of both Maya and Aztec creation narratives, the first people were fashioned from a soft maize dough. In the *Popol Vuh*, the creators Huracán and Gucumatz gave ears of maize to a grandmother goddess Xmucané who ground them to flour, made a paste by mixing it with water and then moulded the first people.

According to Maya folk tradition, the first Mesoamericans were led to identify *teosinte* as a food source when they saw its grains in the dung of a wild cat. The *Popol Vuh* also recorded this debt to animals: Huracán and Gucumatz were led to the discovery of maize by four corn-eating creatures – a coyote, a fox, a parrot and a crow – who had tasted the maize

THE SEARCH FOR FOOD

Mesoamerican creation narratives proposed that before the current world age began there were a number of previous creations. The Aztec account of the five suns or world ages revealed that in each of the five creations the earth's inhabitants found a more satisfactory staple food than eaten by their predecessors.

In the era of the first sun, which was governed by Black Tezcatlipoca, the world was inhabited by a race of giants who lived on acorns. The second sun, whose presiding god was Quetzalcóatl, saw the emergence of a race of primitive humans who lived on the seeds of the mesquite tree.

After the third age, which was ruled by Tláloc, in which people lived on plants that grew on water, such as the water lily, people returned to a diet of wild seeds in the fourth age of Chalchiúhtlicue. It was only in the fifth and current age, an age subject to the sun god Tonatiuh, that the peoples of Mesoamerica learned how to plant and harvest maize.

Above: In a detail from one of the murals in Building A at Cacaxtla, a bird swoops to seize a cocoa pod from a sturdy cacao tree.

and found it good. In Aztec religious narratives, the god Quetzalcóatl – in some accounts, also a culture hero who taught people how to sow and harvest crops – discovered maize deep in the heart of a mountain, where it had been hidden by ants. He was unable to split the mountain to bring the maize to humans, but the god Nanahuatzin – who at the beginning of the current world age rose in the sky to become the sun – broke the peak apart with a thunderbolt.

FIELD AGRICULTURE

Mesoamericans developed different methods of field agriculture in the varied parts of their region. In arid and semi-arid areas fields were laid out where they could be watered by diverted springs and rivers, while in the region of Lake Texcoco farmers developed the technique of building *chinampa*, artificial islands, to reclaim land from the lake. In the dense jungles of the lowlands, fields were cut and the soil enriched by burning vegetation, while in the highlands further south, terraces were carved from the steep slopes.

By 1300BC, the four foods that would become the staple plants of the Mesoamerican civilization were well established in the fields of the pioneer farmers. Together they provided a balanced diet: carbohydrates from maize, protein from beans and squash, oils and fats from avocado. They could be supplemented with meat from rabbits, deer, ducks and geese and with fish.

Below: Cocoa beans are found within cocoa pods, the fruit of the cacao tree. The pods grow on the tree trunk and branches.

CREATING A SACRED WORLD

The oldest religion in Mesoamerica was the cult of the earth's fertility. At the very beginnings of settled life in central America, settlers were fashioning clay female figurines, believed to be representations of an archaic fertility goddess.

MOTHER AND MONSTER

From prehistoric times, Mesoamericans revered the earth as a mother with the capacity to gestate the seeds of domesticated plants and bring forth food. The ancient 260-day ritual calendar celebrated a sacred timespan that was possibly derived from both the lapse between planting and harvest in the Mesoamerican agricultural cycle and the time from conception to

Below: The duality of life and death is represented in a man/skeleton figure made by an Olmec craftsman c.500BC.

birth in a human pregnancy. The earth was a mother, but also a monster. In Aztec religious narrative, the earth monster Tlatecuhtli spread terror in the first days of the current era, when there was nothing but water. She was tamed by the gods Quetzalcóatl and Tezcatlipoca who tore her in two, making the sky from one half and the earth from the other.

OPPOSITES IN BALANCE

Mesoamericans believed the universe to be patterned by duality. Tlatecuhtli consumed the sun god each dusk, consigning him to the underworld for the hours of darkness, but the earth mother then gave birth to the sun once more in the redness of dawn. The earth goddess gave life in the form of crops but also demanded life in the form of sacrificial blood. Mesoamericans saw opposites held in balance. Darkness balancing light, death opposing life, dampness countering dryness, weakness balancing strength.

Duality also structured the divine sphere and was the hidden power of creation. The primal Aztec god Ometeotl ('Lord of Duality') took twin male and female forms, as Tonacatecuhtli ('Lord of our Sustenance') and Tonacacíhuatl ('Lady of our Sustenance') joined in a creative embrace. In Quiché Maya creation narrative, the earth was made when two gods, the sky god Huracán and the sea god Gucumatz came together in discussion. The gods had both benign and threatening aspects: the Maya rain god Chac or the Aztec rain deity Tláloc could deliver drought or lifegiving waters, destructive storms as well as the light moisture falling gently on crops.

The gods also had both spirit forms and physical forms, and most had animal aspects: Mesoamericans viewed the many powerful creatures of their landscape with deep reverence. In one version of the Aztec religious narrative

describing the creation of the sun and moon, the assembled gods who gave of their own blood to set the sun in motion afterwards became the animals of the plains, hills and jungles. The earth was opposed by the heavens, and also balanced the underworld.

In the Mesoamerican vision, the flat earth was both the lowest of the thirteen levels of heaven and the topmost of the nine levels of the underworld. The earth also gave access to the spirit realms of the underworld – the land was marked with sacred caverns that opened the way. The earth was also associated with snakes. According to the Maya, those in a state of religious ecstasy might be delivered

Below: The eagle, symbol of the god Huitzilopochtli and of warrior might, is celebrated on an Aztec wooden drum.

Above: Zoomorph P at Quiriguá shows a young ruler in the jaws of a monster, representing the entry to the underworld.

into the presence of ancestors or the gods by following the coils of a great snake known as the Vision Serpent.

SACRED PATTERNS

For Mesoamericans, the universe was structured according to sacred patterning. One of the forms of this patterning was that of the cyclical movement of time. Mesoamericans believed that everything happened in regular, periodic timespans. For this reason they structured their lives and religious ceremonies around the 260-, 365- and 584-day cycles of the moon, the sun and the planet Venus. Both the Maya and the Aztecs saw the current world as one of a series of creations, subject to periodic destruction and renewal.

In the Aztec view, the present age was the fifth sun or era, and this fivefold pattern was seen also in that of the five directions on the flat earth – north, south, east, west and the centre. In the centre was the great cosmic ceiba tree, and – for the Aztecs – the Templo Mayor of Tenochtitlán. The earth itself was also the centre point of creation, for Mesoamericans believed the earth to be surrounded by water. This gave sacred meaning to the island setting of the Aztecs' imperial capital of Tenochtitlán. The physical characteristics of Mesoamerica informed the range of associations that clustered around the directions of north and south.

To the north of the Valley of Mexico lay desert lands, inhospitable regions from which many nomads, including the México/Aztecs, had escaped. The Aztecs saw the north as a place of dryness and death. It was the direction of the lord of deception and fate, Tezcatlipoca, and was linked to his colour, black – the hue of death. It was associated with xerophyte plants such as the Joshua tree that are adapted to desert climates. In the opposite direction, the south was said by the Aztecs to be the land of dampness, and of their tribal lord Huitzilopochtli, master of the arts of war through which they gathered sacrificial victims. In some versions, the south was the land of the rain god Tláloc, and like his heaven Tlálocan, a place of ease and lifegiving waters.

North and south appear to have been pre-eminent among the four directions. From at least Olmec times in the second millennium BC, many Mesoamerican sites were laid out on a roughly north–south plan. The same pattern was applied in Maya cities such as Tikal and Copán. For the Maya, north was the direction of the celestial realm, home of the gods, and south the way to the underworld. East and west were associated with the daily path of the sun.

Above the earth was the sacred sky, home of the sun god to whom the Aztecs, the people of the sun, dedicated themselves. By night, the movements of the stars followed paths established by the gods in religious and creation narrative. For example, the Great Bear constellation was identified with Tezcatlipoca and its dipping into the sea re-enacted the moment during his struggle with the earth monster at which he lost a foot. The cycle of the planet Venus eternally celebrated the achievements of the Aztec god Quetzalcóatl or the Maya Hero Twins in confronting the lords of the underworld.

In the sacred arenas of their cities, Mesoamericans created idealized versions of their world. Stone pyramids stood for mountains, wide plazas for lakes. Carved stone stelae – known to the Maya as stone trees – honoured the great trunks of the forest. Many scholars believe that the ball court was like a sacred cavern.

Below: This tiny Olmec female figurine was one of many Preclassic Period figures thought to have been used in fertility cults.

THE GLORY OF TEOTIHUACÁN
AD300–500

Teotihuacán continued to expand in size and influence. Thousands of apartment buildings were constructed in the years AD300–500. They were built in compounds, each with room for 60–100 people, probably grouped by kin relationship or craft specialization. Elite dwellings alongside the Street of the Dead were built for higher social groups. The city reached its peak *c.*AD500, with a population of 125,000–200,000. This made it the sixth largest city in the world at the time.

GROWING SPHERE OF INFLUENCE
Some members of this vast population were incomers from other parts of Mesoamerica. One area in the north-eastern part of the city was dubbed the Merchants' Barrio by archaeologists because a large amount of pottery from other Mesoamerican regions was found there. Historians now believe that people from the Gulf coast and the central Maya region made their home there in the years AD300–500. Farther west, another part of the city was home to Zapotec incomers from the Oaxaca region.

Teotihuacán was a major religious centre, built on an ancient sacred site. More than 1,000 shrines and temples lined the Street of the Dead. A large number of full-time priests and temple staff must have resided in the city. Nevertheless, two-thirds of the population were farmers, primarily raising crops of amaranth, maize and squash. Some 9,700 hectares were irrigated, stretching to a distance of around 15km (9 miles) from the city centre. Many artisans and traders lived and worked in the city and its influence – so significant and far-reaching that one could almost speak of an empire – was spread by trade and exchange rather than by war or threat of military force.

The Maya city of Kaminaljuyú in the Guatemala Valley was drawn into Teotihuacán's sphere of influence through trade, probably in obsidian from the

Left: Clay figurines, such as this warrior, were used in religious rites in Teotihuacano homes.

Guatemalan site of El Chayal. In this period, Kaminaljuyú's ceremonial centre was remodelled in the *talud-tablero* (sloping apron/vertical panel) architectural style of Teotihuacán. There might even have been intermarriage between the elites of the two cities. Teotihuacán traders also established a centre at Matacapan in Veracruz in AD400–500.

Monte Albán also continued to thrive, and its population grew. Farmers began to specialize, promoting the growth of a market in agricultural goods. The Zapotecs established a sacred site at Mitla in the Oaxaca region after *c.*AD300. Its name comes from its Aztec Nahuatl name *Mictlan* ('Realm of the Dead').

CENTRAL MAYA REGION
In the central Maya region, the population reached a maximum of about a million by *c.*AD300, after 600 years of steady growth since 300BC. Tikal rose to a pre-eminent position, eclipsing the power of El Mirador.

Many buildings in the North Acropolis were built over earlier constructions between AD250 and AD550. The area was a necropolis celebrating the city's ruling dynasty: eight funerary temples were laid out in a symmetrical pattern on a vast platform of 80m (260ft) by 100m (320ft). Like the structures at Kaminaljuyú, Tikal's buildings show evidence of the influence of Teotihuacano *talud-tablero* architectural style.

A ruler named Yax Moch Xoc was afterwards celebrated at Tikal as the founder of this dynasty. He laid the foundations of Tikal's greatness by establishing the city as an independent ruling centre either through political acumen or military might. His early successors included Moon Zero Bird (whose accession *c.*AD320 and might are celebrated on the jadeite celt known to scholars as the Leyden plaque) and the great king Stormy Sky, whose mortuary shrine was built in Tikal's North Acropolis.

Lowland rivals Tikal and Uaxactún were drawn into increasingly fierce competition that culminated in AD378 when Tikal took control of its rival. A member of the Tikal dynastic elite named Smoking Frog – perhaps the brother of King Great Jaguar Paw – was either installed on the throne at Uaxactún or led a successful war against the city and seized power there. Two carved monuments at each site commemorate the event: bodies found in a tomb at Uaxactún near one of these monuments may be those of the Uaxactún king's family, buried there while the defeated king himself was taken to Tikal for ceremonial slaughter. In the reign of Smoking Frog's successor, Curl Nose, Tikal appears also to have conquered Río Azul c.AD385: altars at Río Azul commemorate the execution of eight local rulers, and Tikal kings are commemorated elsewhere at the site.

Tikal maintained close links to southern Mayan centres, notably Kaminaljuyú. The tomb of the Tikal king Curl Nose, who died c.AD425, contains offerings that prove links with elite burals at Kaminaljuyú. Some scholars have suggested that Curl Nose was a native of Kaminaljuyú who married into the ruling Tikal dynasty. By this route, the influence of Teotihuacán, which was strong at Kaminaljuyú, might have reached Tikal and can be seen in the style of carvings during the reigns of Curl Nose and his son and successor Stormy Sky.

Above: Monte Albán temples use a version of the talud-tablero *(sloping apron/vertical panel) design developed in Teotihuacán.*

Alternatively, there might have been direct trading contacts between Teotihuacán and Tikal. In Stormy Sky's reign, Tikal's power spread further still, to reach Yaxchilán, Quiriguá and even Copán in modern Honduras. A Tikal emblem was carved on a lintel at Yaxchilán c.AD504 and a style associated with Tikal appeared in the carving of monuments at both Copán and Quiriguá during this period.

SOUTHERN MAYA REGION

In the south-east Maya lowlands, Copán in western Honduras became a major centre in the 5th century AD. People had lived in villages in this fertile valley setting since c.1000BC, but the settlement began to expand significantly from c.AD250 onwards. The great dynasty of Copán was founded by Yax Kuk Mo' in AD426. In his reign, the first ritual and administrative buildings were erected at Copán.

Left: Tikal's North Acropolis is one of the city's oldest parts. The towering Temple I (right) was built in the 8th century AD.

POWER CHANGES HANDS
AD500–700

Teotihuacán continued to thrive until *c.*AD550–650, when its vibrant trading network began to fail in the face of competition from the east. In the period up to *c.*AD750, the city maintained a prosperous appearance, despite the fact that decline had set in. The palace of Quetzalpapálotl in the south-west of the Plaza of the Moon, was built after AD500 and the magnificent murals in the Techinantitla apartment building were painted *c.*AD650–750.

Monte Albán expanded greatly in the years AD500–750, covering 6.5km (4 miles) and supporting a population of as many as 24,000.

There were friendly relations between the Zapotec capital and Teotihuacán. Not only were Zapotecs resident in Teotihuacán but, according to carvings on stelae at the South Platform of the Main Plaza at Monte Albán, Teotihuacáno diplomats paid a state visit to the Oaxacan capital.

Below: The Palace of Quetzalpapálotl is an example of the high-status residential and public buildings that continued to be erected in Teotihuacán, despite the city's continuing decline.

Above: This figurine, found in Palenque, represents one of the members of the city's elite group of astronomer-priests.

CENTRAL MAYA REGION

Population of the Maya lowlands in AD500 was an estimated one million, but by *c.*AD600, numbers of people began to climb very significantly, reaching a peak *c.*AD800 of 2.6–3.4 million.

In the first part of this period Tikal continued to thrive. Its success throughout this early-to-mid Classic Period was derived partly from its position: the site was rich in the highly prized natural resource of flint (needed for making chipped stone tools), and lay close to two seasonal swamps or lakes that could be used for intensive farming. The swamps, situated to east and west, helped to make the site easily defensible in times of conflict. Close to rivers that connected it ultimately both to the Gulf and to the Caribbean, Tikal was ideally situated for trade and commerce.

The city appears to have had a vibrant society, with potential for upward movement through military or trading success and this probably helped to inspire its rise and expansion. Tikal was also a major religious centre and place of pilgrimage. It was, finally, one of the pioneers of dynastic kingship in the Maya world. When places such as Calakmul, Yaxchilán, Caracol and Copán were rising to prominence, Tikal was revered as a divinely inspired forerunner.

However, from *c.*AD530, Tikal's position was eclipsed by rivals for a period and its wealth declined severely for about 150 years. Following an attack on Caracol in AD556, in the reign of the Tikal king Double Bird, Tikal was defeated by its rival. A carved ball game marker at Caracol, which archaeologists used to believe was an altar and therefore labelled Altar 21, celebrates the victory of King Lord Water over Tikal in AD562. This probably led to the sacrifice of Double Bird. Tikal entered a period in which its royal burials were far less rich and no significant stelae were erected. The city might well have been diverting much of

Above: Caracol was a major Maya city in Belize. Its core contained 128 plaza groups; the site covered 50sq km (19sq miles).

its wealth to Caracol, which expanded greatly, and Tikal's rulers may have been forbidden by Caracol to erect any stelae.

Refugees from Tikal travelled southwards to the rainforested Petexbatun region close to a major tributary of the Usumacinta river named the Pasión river, where they founded twin capitals at Dos Pilas and Aguateca. The first ruler, Flint Sky, was in power in Dos Pilas in AD647. His emblem glyph was almost identical to that of the Tikal dynasty. Meanwhile, Calakmul in the south-eastern Campeche region of Mexico rose to prominence in the years after AD600 and was an ally of Caracol in wars in the Maya lowlands. With Calakmul's backing, Caracol defeated Naranjo in AD631. Calakmul also entered into alliance with Dos Pilas.

Dos Pilas went on to challenge the formerly mighty Tikal and fought several campaigns, culminating in the defeat of the Tikal ruler Shield Skull by Flint Sky of Dos Pilas in AD679. Flint Sky celebrated his victories in a hieroglyphic stairway at Dos Pilas. However, Tikal's pride was to be reborn. In AD695, King

Ah Cacau of Tikal captured and sacrificed Jaguar Paw-Jaguar of Calakmul. Meanwhile, in the south-western Maya lowlands, Palenque established itself as a major power and the dominant force in the region in the early 7th century AD. Inscriptions at the site provide a long dynastic list, going back as far as the probable founder, Balam Kuk, who came to the throne in AD431 and even further beyond to an assuredly mythical figure named Kin Chan, who was said to have come to the throne in 967BC. However, the city's great success coincided with the long and stable reign of King Pacal, whose splendid tomb would be laid beneath the Temple of Inscriptions in his city. Pacal came to the throne in AD615 and the earliest surviving use of the Palenque emblem glyph is dated to his reign.

SOUTHERN MAYA REGION
Kaminaljuyú thrived greatly by trade in obsidian, but began to decline after AD550, perhaps because the waning of Teotihuacán affected trade. The settlements of the Guatemala Valley became markedly less prosperous and were abandoned altogether by c.AD800, as their inhabitants retreated to more easily fortified and defended hilltop positions.

Copán greatly expanded its sphere of influence, particularly in the long reigns of Butz' Chan (AD578–628) and Smoke Jaguar (AD628–95). In this time of great dynastic strength and stability, Copán took control of Quiriguá in AD653 and of much of the valley of the Motagua river, and thus of the trade in jade and obsidian that travelled down that corridor from the highlands to the Caribbean sea.

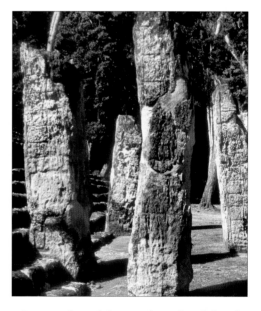

Above: Stelae celebrate rulers of Calakmul in south-eastern Campeche. Calakmul was at least as large as its famed rival Tikal.

49

THE COLLAPSE OF SOCIAL ORDER
AD700–900

In the years after AD700, Teotihuacán continued its slow collapse in prestige and power as the city's merchants endured the decay of the trade network that had once connected them to Veracruz, Tikal, the Guatemala Valley and beyond. After a fire c.AD750, the centre was abandoned, but about 40,000 people continued to live in outlying parts of the city. Monte Albán declined at the same time, beginning c.AD750, as the people of the Oaxaca valleys turned to local centres such as Lambityeco and Jalieza rather than the regional capital for the focus of their ritual life and work. Monte Albán's hilltop was abandoned and its population declined to about 4,000 by AD900.

The collapse of the centuries-old social order embodied by large centres such as Teotihuacán created a period of flux and of military conflict between small kingdoms. Peoples competed for trade and pre-eminence: many groups were on the move in the 7th, 8th and 9th centuries, leading to shifts in balance of

Below: Xochicalco and El Tajín were among the centres that rose to prominence with the decline of Teotihuacán and Monte Albán.

power and the emergence of new settlements. A Maya group named the Olmeca-Xicalanga travelled westwards from southern Veracruz and Tabasco to establish their capital in the fortress of Cacaxtla, on a hilltop dominating the Tlaxcala Valley, some time after AD650. The city, renowned for its murals, was at its peak until AD900. Settlements were established at Azcopatzalco, Cerro Portesuelo, Xico and Cerro de la Estrella in the Valley of Mexico.

To the south of the Valley of Mexico the fortified city of Xochicalco, in the western part of the Morelos region, won itself a regional state reaching west into the Balsas Depression, north into the Ajusco Mountains and south-west into the region known as Mixteca Baja. Xochicalco, although occupied in the previous centuries, was at its height in the years c.AD700–900.

In the tropical rainforest of northern Veracruz, El Tajín became an important centre. The site had been settled as early as c.AD100 and had thrived by contact with Teotihuacán: as Teotihuacáno influence waned, El Tajín began to assert its authority over its region. The same

Above: Carved columns on the roof of the Temple of the Warriors, Chichén Itzá, once supported the roof. The Castillo is beyond.

process – of increasing independence following the decline of Teotihuacán – applied to Cholula (in modern Puebla) and other city-states.

THE RISE OF THE ITZÁ
Other Maya groups known as the Chontal-speaking Maya, the Putún and the Itzá spread out from a base in the region of Chontalapa, in northern coastal Tabasco and south-western Campeche, at the western edge of the Yucatán peninsula. They were warrior-merchants, seeking political control and wealth through trade. Some established themselves at Palenque in the 7th to 9th centuries, others moved inland along the Usumacinta river to Yaxchilán, Altar de Sacrificios and Seibal. Putún Maya may have travelled into the southern Maya region along the upper reaches of the Usumacinta in the northern highlands.

The Itzá moved up the western coast of the Yucatán peninsula, then went inland towards the cities of Uxmal and Chichén Itzá. Most historians believe that the Itzá were established in Chichén Itzá by AD850. Inscriptions on important buildings at Chichén Itzá raised in the years AD869–81 praise an early Itzá leader named Kakupacal, who claimed to be related to the dynasty of Palenque.

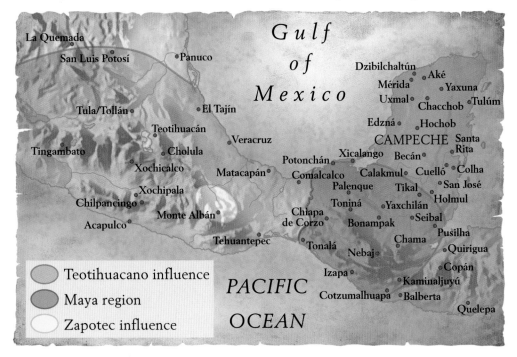

La Quemada
San Luis Potosí • Panuco
Gulf of Mexico
Dzibilchaltún
Aké
Mérida • Yaxuna
Tula/Tollán • El Tajín
Uxmal • Chacchob Tulúm
Teotihuacán
Edzná • Hochob
Veracruz
Tingambato • Cholula
CAMPECHE Santa Rita
Xicalango Becán
Xochicalco Potonchán
Matacapán Comalcalco Calakmul • Cuelló • Colha
Xochipala Palenque Tikal • San José
Chilpancingo Toniná • Yaxchilán Holmul
Monte Albán Chiapa de Corzo Bonampak • Seibal
Acapulco
Tehuantepec Tonalá Chama Pusilha
Nebaj • Quirigua
Izapa Copán
PACIFIC Kaminaljuyú
Cotzumalhuapa • Balberta
OCEAN Quelepa

🔵 Teotihuacano influence
🔵 Maya region
⚪ Zapotec influence

CENTRAL MAYA REGION

In the Petexbatun region, Dos Pilas built a short-lived empire through warfare and diplomacy. After the death of the city's founder, Flint Sky, his son – known to historians as Shield God K – took power in AD698 and entered an alliance with Naranjo. His successor, who is known only as Ruler 3, defeated Seibal in AD735, made a marriage alliance with Cancuén and was also allied to the great power of Caracol. His successor, Ruler 4, extended the empire to cover c.4,000km (2,500 miles), but in AD761 he was captured and beheaded by a rival lord at Tamarindito. The power at the centre was gone and the area plunged into bitter conflict. Dos Pilas was largely abandoned after the AD761 war.

Palenque was at war with the city of Toniná in the Ocosingo Valley in the early 8th century. King Kan Xul II of Palenque was captured and beheaded by the ruler of Toniná in AD711.

In the Maya lowlands, Tikal enjoyed a great renaissance after more than 150 years in which it had erected no stelae and apparently suffered a severe decline in wealth. King Ah Cacau restored the city's military and political standing abroad by defeating the rival city of Calakmul and embarked on major building projects at home, including the erection of Temples I and II.

THE MAYA COLLAPSE

In the late 8th and 9th centuries the city-states of the Maya lowlands one by one stopped erecting stelae celebrating their divine kings. The cities fell into decline before being finally abandoned altogether. Historians believe that the decline was caused by a chain of events kick-started by overpopulation in the region, which led to ever more intensive farming and the degradation of the environment, matched by a fiercer form of warfare that focused less on raiding for prestige and more on territorial expansion. The result

was population decline – numbers in the southern lowlands fell by one-third in the century after AD830. Several sites – including Piedras Negras, Quiriguá, Naranjo and Calakmul – erected their last stela in AD810. The last carved stela was raised at Caracol in AD859 and at Tikal in AD869.

At Tikal, as at Dos Pilas and many other formerly magnificent centres, the cities were invaded by squatters who eked out a living in thatched homes on the great ceremonial plazas: they were not afraid to move monuments and even break into the tombs of once great kings in search of riches. However, this collapse

Above: A Cacaxtla mural figure showing a man transformed into a jaguar, c.AD900.

did not take effect farther east in coastal or riverside settlements in Belize, where Rita Caracol, Lamanai and other sites continued to thrive after AD900.

Quiriguá in the Motagua Valley had been subject to Copán since AD653, but rose to challenge its overlord. In AD738 Cauac Sky of Quiriguá beheaded King 18 Rabbit of Copán. In this way, Quiriguá gained control of the lucrative trade in obsidian, jade and other items passing from the Guatemalan highlands along the Motagua valley.

51

THE TRIUMPH OF THE TOLTECS
AD900–1200

The city of Tollán (modern Tula) in the state of Hidalgo took over from Teotihuacán as the pre-eminent centre of highland Mexico c.AD950. It stood on a ridge overlooking a tributary of the Pánuco river named the Tula, near to the northern limit of Mesoamerica. It ruled for more than 200 years.

HOME OF THE TOLTECS
The Aztecs and early chroniclers wove a web of religious narrative around the origins of this city, home to the Toltecs so revered by the Méxica of Tenochtitlán and also to the great feathered serpent god, Quetzalcóatl. According to this narrative, Quetzalcóatl or Ce Acatl Topiltzin was the son of a leader of the Chichimec people, who left his home at

Above: Each of the temple-top figures at Tollán (Tula) wears warrior garb: a butterfly breastplate and feathered headdress.

Below: Towering carved warriors facing west atop the Temple of Tlahuizcalpantecuhtli at Tollán (Tula) proclaim Toltec might.

Culhuacán in the Valley of Mexico to assume leadership of the Toltec community of Tollán. Here he presided over a wondrous age of artistic expression and scientific achievement, but a Toltec named Huastec – in conjunction with Tezcatlipoca, god of darkness and fate – brought disgrace upon Ce Acatl Topiltzin, who departed from the city. Different versions recount that he either cast himself on a sacrificial pyre and rose into the heavens as the planet Venus or that he sailed away to the east on a raft of snakes, promising to return.

Historians do not know for sure who the Toltec founders of Tollán were. The evidence suggests that they were warlike incomers from the north.

The city they built covered 13sq km (8sq miles) and was home to a population of up to 60,000 people. It was a centre for craftspeople working obsidian, making pots, stoneware and tools from chert. The ritual centre – consisting of two plazas, two pyramids, meeting halls and two ball courts – was oriented precisely 18 degrees east of true north.

From Tollán the Toltecs exerted control over – and probably received tribute from – a sizeable area, incorporating the northern part of the Valley of Mexico, the region of modern Hidalgo state as far east as Tulancingo, plus the Toluca Valley, areas of the Bajío and territories around the Lerma River. The empire's days of glory were numbered, however, and the city was overrun and burned c.1150–1200.

In the period of Tollán's pre-eminence, the settlement of Cholula in the Puebla region of Mexico was also thriving. The town's wealth and prestige were such that its pyramid was rebuilt to a height of 55m (180ft). Historians are uncertain whether Cholula was a rival or an ally of Tollán.

CHICHÉN ITZÁ
Another legend concerning the Toltecs suggests that a group from Tollán led by Quetzalcóatl travelled to the Gulf Coast in the 10th century and then under the

Above: The six tiers and crowning temple of the Pyramid of the Niches, El Tajín, were built over a similar earlier version of the building.

leadership of Kukulcán (the Maya form of Quetzalcóatl) made their way to northern Yucatán, where they settled in Chichén Itzá. Many elements of Toltec/Mexican style in architecture and religious iconography appeared at Chichén Itzá; these were most likely spread through trade.

Chichén Itzá was by now the heart of a growing tributary empire. The Tutil Xiu, an Itzá elite and ruling dynasty, grew wealthy by trading in salt from the Yucatán salt beds, in obsidian, which they imported from Mexico, in ceramics and in basalt. They developed port facilities on Ilsa Cerritos, an island just off the northern coast of Yucatán. They ruled through a group of nobles rather than

through a single, divinely blessed king. However, the Itzá apparently made many enemies, for native chronicles contain many slighting references to these successful incomers. Around 1100, the city of Mayapán was founded around 100km (80 miles) to the west of Chichén Itzá and quickly became its principal rival.

A NICHE IN VERACRUZ

El Tajín continued to thrive in northern Veracruz. Its six-tier Pyramid of the Niches is an elaborate variation on Teotihuacáno *talud-tablero* architectural style. The site also contains no fewer than 12 ball courts: the city may have been a centre for playing the game and could have hosted regional competitions. There is even the possibility that many centuries before El Tajín's independent glory, the ball game could have been developed in this part of Mesoamerica.

SOUTHERN MAYA LANDS

In the period of Chichén Itzá's glory, northern raiders appear to have brought terror to Southern Maya regions, where many settlements on valley floors were abandoned as people moved to easily defensible hilltop settings, and built ditches, walls and other fortifications. These incomers came either from northern Yucatán or from the Gulf Coast region of Chontalapa. They brought their architectural style and warrior imagery along with them.

A settlement at Chuitinamit-Atitlan on Lake Atitlan has a carving of a feathered serpent mouth opening to release human heads that is reminiscent of imagery at Chichén Itzá. Another at Chalchitan, on the Uscaminta tributary the Chixoy, contains a platform that may be a Chichén Itzá-style skull rack or *tzom-pantli*, on which skulls were displayed.

BY CANOE AND PADDLE

In the 10th century, the powerful merchants of Chichén Itzá built a trading post on Isla Cerritos, a small island just off the coast of northern Yucatán and about 90km (55 miles) from their capital city. They built or improved existing piers and docks, together with a 330m (1,000ft) sea wall to guarantee calm waters for unloading from large seagoing canoes. These vessels, recently developed, transformed seagoing trade. At 15m (50ft) long and 2m (6ft 6in) wide, they were far bigger than earlier canoes and able to voyage into far rougher waters.

SEA TRADE

Through Isla Cerritos, Chichén Itzá imported basalt from Belize, gold jewellery from Central America, pottery from Guatemala and obsidian from sites in Mexico. Itzá sea traders travelled as far as the ports of Naco and Nito in Honduras.

Coastal settlements were probably operated in this way as trading posts for powerful inland cities or states throughout Mesoamerican history. For example, Cerros, on a peninsula of coastal Belize

Below: Caribbean waves wash the shore by the trading centre of Cozumel. Goats were traded by canoe along the coast and among offshore islands.

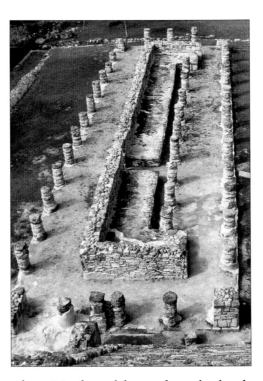

Above: Members of the merchant elite lived in the Palace of the Kings, a sumptuous residence in the trading city of Mayapán.

that projects into Chetumal Bay, was transformed from a small village into a significant settlement with large pyramids, public buildings and platforms in the period 50BC–AD100, probably at the behest of an inland centre seeking an outlet into the Caribbean Sea. The style

and appearance of the stucco deity-masks on these buildings suggest links to nearby Lamanai or, farther afield, to Tikal. Archaeological evidence has led historians to suggest that Cerros operated in tandem with Komchen, far away in northern Yucatán, as a trading partner, probably in the movement of salt from the northern region. Jade and obsidian from the southern Maya region were also traded at Cerros.

Mesoamericans carried on sea trade from earliest times. The peoples of western Mexico were in contact along the Pacific coast with tribes in Ecuador as early as 1500BC – as suggested by the appearance of Ecuadorian-style chamber tombs. In the Olmec centre at Teopantecuanitlán, in the Guerrero region, a workshop produced elite items using marine shells from distant points on the Pacific Coast.

TRADING POSTS

Many sites along the coasts of the Yucatán peninsula and Belize thrived through seagoing trade for many centuries. Jaina Island, the settlement off the west coast of the peninsula celebrated for its cemetery and the clay figures left in its graves, was a thriving trading and fishing port for at least 700 years. Tancah, a fortified town on the eastern coast of northern Yucatán,

Above: The elite of Yucatán combined warfare with trade. This is a mural in the Temple of the Warriors in Chichén Itzá.

appears to have been a centre for trade in the *Strombus gigas*, a type of conch shell used in religious ritual from at least the time of Teotihuacán, where the shells are depicted in murals. Tancah was a trading post from the last centuries BC onwards, handling obsidian, jade, pyrite, granite and slate vessels exported from the Maya cities of the Puuc region inland. The neighbouring coastal settlement of Xelha was a port for the inland city of Cobá from at least the 10th century. A *sacbé* or raised causeway left the main square of Xelha and ran inland to Cobá.

CONTROL OF SEA TRADE

Around 6km (3½ miles) south along the coast lay Tulum, which was founded on the cliff top overlooking the Caribbean Sea in 1200 at a time when maritime commerce was a source of great wealth and prestige for the merchants of the northern Yucatán peninsula.

A cliff-top beacon guided sailors through a gap in the reef that runs parallel to the shore and on to a safe landing on the beach beneath the town. At this time, the cities of the League of

Mayapán – Mayapán, Uxmal and a Chichén Itzá much reduced from its former independent glory – had control of seagoing trade, and probably built Tulum.

The League's merchant elite also maintained an offshore trading centre on the Isle of Cozumel, a little further north opposite the mainland settlement of Xcaret. On Cozumel, large platforms right across the island were used as seasonal stores for products such as honey, cacao and salt. The island traded all year in obsidian and building stone. The western part of Cozumel was the site of one of the region's most important religious shrines, to the Maya Moon Goddess Ix Chel.

Below: Lying in the sacred east, Tulum – together with Xelhá and Tancah – was a religious as well as a trading site. This structure is a clifftop temple to the wind god.

TRADERS, SPIES, PROTECTORS

Long-range trade in the Aztec empire was handled by professional merchants called *pochteca*. Working both on their own behalf and as emissaries of rulers and members of the nobility, they specialized in importing luxurious materials such as animal skins, rare feathers, precious shells and stones used in religious ritual. The Aztec word *pochteca* is derived from their name for the *Bombax ceiba*, the great tropical tree that was viewed by the ancient Mesoamericans as the tree of life that linked the terrestrial realm to heaven and to the underworld. The tree of life was an image for the king or rule, and the association of *pochteca* with the tree suggests that merchants were viewed – like kings – as protectors or guarantors of stability and fertility.

MERCHANT WARDS

Pochteca were an elite hereditary group, whose members lived together as a *capultin* kin body in a part of the city reserved for them. Such was the size of Tenochtitlán and the number of *pochteca* serving the empire that there were six wards for merchants in the capital: Amachtlan, Atlauhco, Itztotolco, Pochtlán, Tepetitlán and Tzonmolco.

Ten other towns in the Valley of Mexico were renowned for their communities of professional merchants. These were: Azcapotzalco, Chalco, Coatlinchán, Cuauhtitlán, Huexotla, Huitzilopochco, Otumba, Mixcoac, Texcoco and Xochimilco.

There was a strict hierarchy among *pochteca*. The *pochtecatlatoque* were the most senior merchants, handpicked by the *tlatoani* and his advisers to organize

Left: This exquisite jade ear ornament, carved delicately with Maya glyphs, was found by archaeologists at Pomona, Belize.

trading expeditions and to supervize the activities of younger traders. They were proven merchants with wide experience of travel, usually drawn from the 'aristocracy' of trading families. The *pochtecatlatoque* stayed in Tenochtitlán and followed the progress of an expedition through reports sent back by the travelling merchants; both overseer and trader took a share in the profits. Perhaps most prestigious of all the responsibilities of the *pochtecatlatoque* was to ensure that the capital's markets were orderly and honest places. They sat in judgement on dishonest *pochteca* and customers in special merchants' courts and no other authority could interfere with or challenge their judgements. A trader found guilty of cheating or selling stolen goods or a person caught trying to steal would be sentenced to death.

SLAVE TRADERS

Second in the hierarchy of *pochteca* were traders in slaves. They were called *tlaltlani* ('washers of slaves'), a reference to the ritual bathing that slaves underwent before they were taken to be sacrificed. Bernardino de Sahagún recounts in his *General History of the Things of New Spain* that *tlaltlani* were the wealthiest of all merchants. By tradition they were particularly devout and were treated with the greatest respect as providers of sacrificial victims.

Beneath them were the travelling *pochteca*, the veterans of long-range expeditions who brought luxury produce back to Tenochtitlán's eager markets. They were sometimes called *oztomeca* ('front-line merchants'). Those among the *oztomeca* who worked only for the *tlatoani* were called *tencunenenque* ('king's voyagers'); they often worked as collectors of tribute from subject states within the empire.

Pochteca held a special position of privilege. Unlike their fellows, they were not required to perform personal services for the *tlatoani*. Instead they provided elite goods as tribute. In 1500, as a reward for the role played by *pochteca* in the military conquest of Soconusco, the *tlatoani* Ahuítzotl (*r.* 1486–1502) made a proclamation praising long-range merchants and granting them the right to wear loincloths and capes that were normally reserved for the nobility on special occasions.

SPIES BEHIND ENEMY LINES

One group of merchants, the *naualoztomeca* ('traders in disguise'), performed a vital function for the *tlatoani*, his military advisers and the army commanders. Wherever they went, ostensibly travelling as merchants, they were working as spies, looking for signs of potential unrest and listening for mutterings of discontent against the Aztec rulers. When the military elite in Tenochtitlán was planning a military campaign, it would send *naualoztomeca* into the region to seek useful preliminary information.

In the early Aztec era, traveller-spies went through the empire disguised as locals in order to learn what they could from gossip in the marketplace. However, later the travellers began to take the guise of merchants. It was a dangerous occupation; if caught, a spy was likely to be slain and perhaps cooked. Upon landing in Mexico, Hernán Cortés made first contact with a group of *naualoztomeca*. It was these trader-spies who carried the first news of strange bearded beings in 'flying' ships back to the court of Moctezuma II in Tenochtitlán.

NOBLE MAYA TRADERS

The Aztecs' Maya contemporaries did not have professional merchants comparable to the *pochteca*. Among the Maya, long-distance trade was carried out by rulers and members of the nobility. At Chichén Itzá and Mayapán, the rulers appear to have been merchants. One account of the fall of Mayapán recounts that all the city's rulers were slaughtered in an attack, save one who was away from the city on his travels, seeking trade.

In both Maya and Aztec lands, short-distance trading was performed either by small-scale entrepreneurs, peddlers who bought and sold as they travelled hither and

Right: Danger on the road. A detail from the Codex Mendoza *shows Aztec trader-spies being attacked by lawless locals.*

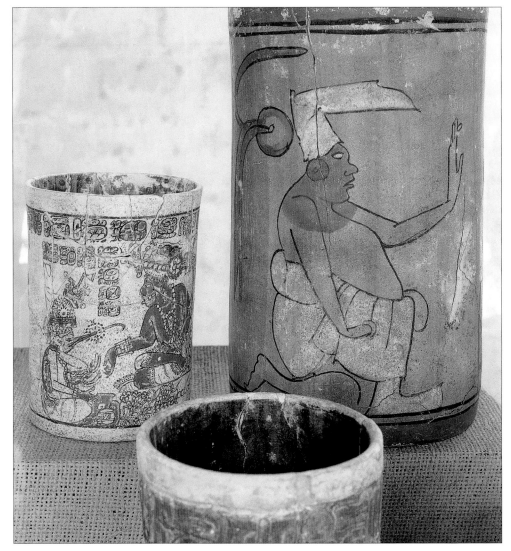

thither, or by the producers and manufacturers of the goods – the farmers, weavers, toolmakers and potters. From ancient times, across Mesoamerica, long-distance trade was the preserve of a wealthy ruling elite. Trade was the lifeblood of development: because they brought wealth to the community, and because they traded in

Above: The largest of these vases from Tikal shows a fat Maya merchant who was clearly wealthy enough to indulge himself.

elite goods such as feathers, jaguar skins and sacrificial knives that were needed for religious ceremony, traders began to enjoy religious prestige.

MARKETS LARGE AND SMALL

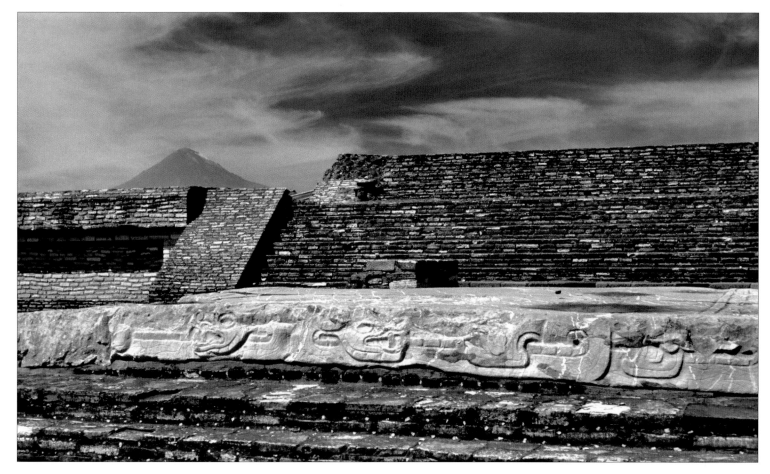

The Aztec capital contained several outdoor markets of various sizes. (The outdoor marketplace was called *tianquiztli* in Nahuatl.) In addition to the justly celebrated marketplace in Tlatelolco, there was another substantial market in Tenochtitlán proper, alongside the ceremonial precinct. There were also many smaller places of sale scattered throughout the city in its various wards.

WHO SOLD WHAT, WHEN
The sale of elite goods that had been transported from distant parts of the empire was probably restricted to the Tlatelolco and the main Tenochtitlán market. Sales in the different wards were probably of local agricultural produce brought in from *chinampa* fields or of craft products made at workshops in the vicinity. Transactions at these markets were not purely economic, but were bound into the fabric of life and

Above: The walls, steps and frieze carving are part of the vast Pyramid of Quetzalcóatl in Cholula, a town sacred to that god.

Right: These steps and walls are another part of the pyramid remains at Cholula, a major trading as well as a religious centre.

intimately connected with entertainment, socializing, politics and religion. Markets were places where people made friends, swapped news and gossip, perhaps hatched plots and formed alliances, places through which people made their way to the temple.

It is possible that market days were scheduled to coincide with important days in the ritual calendar. Pilgrims would have travelled to a town to make offerings at its shrine and then gone on to the marketplace. Merchants would have taken part in the pilgrimage.

RELIGION AND COMMERCE

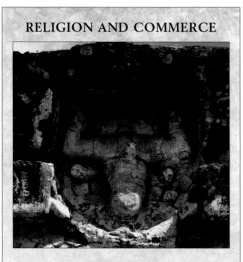

Above: The Descending God, Tulum.

Many Mesoamerican trading settlements were also important religious centres. In the highlands of Mexico, Cholula's marketplace was thronged with people while the city's great Temple of Quetzalcóatl was a major draw for pilgrims.

Several trading sites on the eastern seaboard of the Yucatán peninsula were believed to have sacred power because of their position towards the direction of the moon's rising and the reappearance of Venus. The Isle of Cozumel, an important trading port for the League of Mayapán, contained a shrine to moon goddess Ix Chel on its eastward-facing shore; the goddess was believed to speak through an oracle there. On the mainland, the fortified trading centre at Tancah was the site of a *cenote* or large natural well with a holy cave lying on an east–west axis and painted with murals delineating the fearful power of the sea. At nearby Tulum, the Temple of the Descending God was adorned with a carving of a creature diving towards earth; the curious image, only found at Tulum and Cobá, is thought to be associated with the cult of the planet Venus in the form of Xux Ek, the Maya 'wasp star' god.

It is likely that the holy day was enjoyed as a holiday, with entertainments and perhaps a ball game tournament.

Some markets specialized in local produce. Cholula, for example, won a wide reputation for the excellence of its chillies, while Coyoacán was known for the wood grown near the town. Fine gourds, cloth and ceramics were the speciality of Texcoco market. The best places to go for slaves were Azcapotzalco and Itzocán, and the best dog market was at Acolman. In the Mixtec area, the market at Miahuatlán was widely renowned, not least for its sale of exquisite local gold work. Smaller markets were usually held each day or sometimes on a rota with other nearby centres.

MAYA MARKETS

Many Maya towns and cities also held centralized markets in open squares. There is little archaeological evidence of marketplaces, however. Commercial activity usually took place in the open, with perhaps a few pole-and-thatch buildings to provide shade or to keep the rain off, that have since decayed. There is evidence that Classic Period Tikal had a permanent central marketplace. Archaeologists believe that the commercial zone was probably an enclosed area of the city's East Plaza, containing buildings with many doorways. We know that in the post-Classic Period, Iximche in the southern Maya region had a market plaza with overseers to settle arguments, ensure that regulations were observed and levy taxes. As at Tlatelolco, Maya markets were efficiently organized, with different types of goods laid out in separate areas.

Markets contained areas for visiting and foreign merchants, but rival controlling interests sometimes came into opposition. For example, Aztec *pochteca* trading in elite goods were not welcome in areas where Maya nobles ran long-distance trade. Where necessary, representatives of the two sides met in neutral areas.

Below: At Tollán, the remains of the Palacio Quemado lie to the west of the raised temple platform sacred to Quetzalcóatl.

A NETWORK OF TRIBUTE

Large quantities of produce entered Tenochtitlán in the form of tribute payments from provinces within the Aztec empire. The activities of tribute collectors complemented those of *pochteca* merchants in providing sumptuous goods to please the nobles of the imperial capital and to supply the materials used in the city's magnificent religious ceremonies.

A TRIBUTARY EMPIRE

Some *pochteca* worked as itinerant tribute collectors, but generally collectors were appointed to reside in a conquered territory to ensure payments were made. The Triple Alliance of Tenochtitlán, Texcoco and Tlacopán built its tributary empire through military might: its armies pursued battle to the point at which a conquered state or city agreed to pay tribute, when the conquerors imposed a schedule of amounts and timings. The rulers of the defeated state remained in power, and the collector made sure that they honoured the tribute agreement, under threat of further military action.

Tribute payments maintained the infrastructure and daily operations of the empire. Some provinces were required to send labourers for construction projects, others tools and building materials, some

Below: The Zapotecs of Monte Albán celebrated their conquest-led tribute network in carvings on the arrow-shaped Building J.

sent soldiers, others military equipment such as shields and padded cotton war jerkins. Many areas sent maize, beans and other basic foodstuffs, while others provided firewood for the braziers of the nobility. Certain states were contracted to send local products such as obsidian or cacao, fine metalwork or ceramics, jaguar skins or colourful feathers. One of the most highly prized Aztec tributary provinces was the resource-rich region of Soconusco, defeated after four years' conflict by Ahuítzotl in 1486; it provided tribute of jaguar skins and jewellery.

RECORDS OF PAYMENT

Details of the tribute network operated by Texcoco are found in the 16th-century document the *Mapa Quinatzin*. They show how meticulously tribute operations were planned. There were eight tributary regions, each with its own tribute collector required, among other responsibilities, to furnish the administrative buildings, city temples and royal palaces in Texcoco with foodstuffs and wood for braziers. In particular, two groups of 13 tributary towns were arranged in a rota to provide firewood for the *tlatoani*'s main palace throughout the year. The *Codex Mendoza* (*c*.1541) contains a lengthy tribute list detailing the responsibilities throughout the year of various tributary towns and states. Cuauhnahuac is listed as one of 16 towns contracted to dispatch a consignment of cotton skirts, loincloths and robes to Tenochtitlán twice a year, supplemented by an annual delivery of shields and war equipment. With so many tribute payers required to provide materials according to a regular schedule, there must have been a steady stream of porters and canoes bringing deliveries from far and wide, which would have required detailed administrative control.

Before the Triple Alliance, other cultures – including the Zapotecs of Monte Albán and the Toltecs of Tollán – established tributary empires. At Monte

Above: Portable wealth. This pendant earring of solid gold was one of the pieces found in Monte Albán Tomb 7 in 1932.

Right: A page from the Codex Mendoza *shows the tribute collected by Aztec civil servants from the province of Tochtepec.*

Albán, the curious arrow-shaped structure known to archaeologists as Building J, erected between *c.*200BC and AD300 in the Main Plaza, bears about 50 carvings that appear to represent areas conquered or required to pay tribute to the Zapotecs. Some carvings specify the kind of tribute that must be paid.

They included Cuicatlán, a mountain settlement on the border between Oaxaca and the Téhuacan Valley, and Tututepec on the coast of the Pacific Ocean. At Cuicatlán the Zapotecs acted with great ruthlessness: they destroyed entire villages, moved other settlements, established military strongholds and terrified surviving locals by building skull racks in their villages to display the heads of their conquered menfolk.

In many areas they did not need to use military force, however. In return for supplying elite goods from Monte Albán to the leading figures of a village, the Zapotecs exacted an agreement that they would receive tribute of agricultural produce. Many centuries later, the warriors of Xochicalco, in the western part of Morelos, established a tributary empire in the period AD700–900, as evidenced by glyphs of tribute-paying towns carved on the upper part of the Pyramid of the Feathered Serpent there.

The Putún Maya traders who ruled Chichén Itzá and later Mayapán both built tribute networks. At Mayapán, cotton, copal, cacao, honey and turkeys were among the forms of tribute received. In the southern Maya realm the warlike Quiché Maya also exacted tribute payments from those they conquered. However, the Quiché did not allow local leaders to remain in place, as the Aztecs did; instead, triumphant warlords had their enemies executed and took the dead men's wives into their own families.

THE GIVING OF GIFTS

From earliest times goods moved across Mesoamerica in the form of gifts between elite groups in different areas. Such gift-giving was a mark of mutual respect between rulers and a way of sharing resources between regions rich in different source materials – for instance, a highland group might make a gift of obsidian cutting blades in return for surplus maize or cacao grown by another group in the coastal lowlands. The gift of sumptuous and prestigious materials was also a statement of power on behalf of the giver, an attempt to demonstrate status. Moctezuma II attempted to prove his divine grandeur and magnificence by making splendid gifts of gold, silver and magnificent featherwork to Hernán Cortés and the conquistadors in 1519.

THE SACRED WAY

The Maya built raised causeways known as *sacbeob* (singular: *sacbé*) between settlements. These paved roads eased communications and passage for merchants while giving solid form to political alliances among cities.

GREAT CAUSEWAY

The greatest of these roads was built *c*.AD800 in Yucatán, and ran for 100km (60 miles) from the Castillo pyramid at Cobá to Yaxuná. Cobá lay at the intersection of some 43 roads. It was also connected, for example, to its seaport at Xelhá. Some scholars believe that the rulers of Cobá embarked on this remarkable feat of engineering in an attempt to consolidate their power at a time when the aggressive Putún Maya incomers at Chichén Itzá were making unwelcome intrusions into the region. The attempt may have succeeded: the Itzá attacked and defeated Yaxuná in *c*.AD850, but there is no evidence they overcame Cobá. Its people maintained their independence, although the city's trading success was limited, its ambitious building programmes were curtailed and various outer parts of the settlement were gradually abandoned.

Several *sacbeob* were constructed in northern Yucatán. Typically they were elevated 2.5m (8ft) above the surround-

Left: A sacbé connects a small group of buildings to the two-storey palace at Labná. The palace is similar to that at Sayil.

ing land, were around 4.5m (15ft) wide and covered with lime cement. Labourers used a 5-ton roller to finish the surface; this would have needed 15 workers to push it. The roads did not curve: they ran perfectly straight, then made a sudden turn to change direction if necessary. One – 4m (13ft) wide – ran for 18km (11 miles) between Uxmal and Kabah. At Kabah it passed through a remarkable stone corbelled arch with a span of 5m (16ft) and led to the central civic area. Another ran for 18km from the settlement at Ucí. It was a remarkable 8m (26ft) wide.

The Maya built *sacbeob* from the time they erected their first monumental buildings in the lowlands. The earliest known system links El Mirador to Nakbé, 13km (8 miles) away, Tintal and other nearby sites. These roads were built in the Late Preclassic Period (*c*.400BC–AD250). The *sacbeob* between cities were expanded versions of the sacred ways that the Maya built to link areas within their

Above: Several causeways were in use at the fortified trading centre at La Quemada in Zacatecas state, Mexico.

cities. At El Mirador, causeways connected different parts of the city centre. A series of *sacbeob* ran from the Great Plaza in the centre of Tikal. One led north, to the buildings labelled Pyramid Group 3D-2 and Group H by archaeologists. Another went directly west to Temple IV and a third ran south-east to the Temple of Inscriptions. At Chichén Itzá a stone *sacbé* 6m (20ft) wide and 300m (985ft) long connected the Temple of the Feathered Serpent to the Sacred cenote.

SACRED SYMBOLISM

The causeways in cities such as Tikal were integrated into the sacred symbolism of the site layout. The arcane meaning of the layout was that the north was the realm of supernaturals, glorious deceased ancestors who had risen to the heavens, while the south was the region of the Underworld. A ball court was often built between north and south to represent an entrance to the Underworld. Buildings to the east and west suggested the east–west passage of the sun and the rule of the king, whose symbol was the sun.

Causeways were used to link different symbolic areas and to emphasize the unity of the design. At Tikal, for example, the sacred north position was filled both by the North Acropolis, which contained many tombs of ancestors, and further out by the Pyramid Group 3D-2. South was the South Acropolis, west was Temple IV and east was the Temple of the Inscriptions. The three causeways completed the design. A ball court in the East Plaza was an additional way into the Underworld between north and south.

In many cities, for example Yaxhá and Caracol, causeways were built to lead out from the centre to outer settlements. At Caracol there were no fewer than seven causeways providing access from the centre to living areas and plazas, with one running for 8km (5 miles) to the allied smaller settlement at Cahal Pichik. At Seibal the three main groups of buildings were laid out on a cluster of hilltops and connected to one another by causeways. A few *sacbeob* were built in other parts

Below: Archaeologists have dated this well-preserved roadway at Cantona in Puebla state to AD700–950.

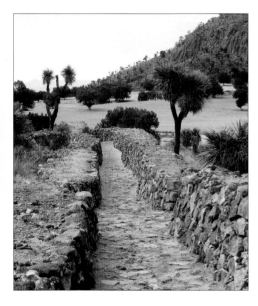

of Mesoamerica. At Xochicalco, paved causeways like *sacbeob* were the connecting link between different parts of the ancient city. In northern Mexico the trading settlement of La Quemada, in southern Zacatecas state, also used causeways to link different parts of the settlement.

AZTEC ROADS
There is little archaeological evidence of Aztec roads. Whereas in Maya lands labourers built paved *sacbeob*, in southern and central highland Mesoamerica there was generally no need to build formal roads between settlements. However, scholars know that a network of routes carried trade within the Aztec empire.

Above: The carving on the façade of the Governor's Palace at Uxmal is reproduced in Catherwood's 1841 drawing. From Uxmal a sacbé *ran directly to Kabah, where it passed beneath an archway.*

There are references in post-Conquest accounts to roads, roadside gods, rest houses and teams of couriers and there was certainly a road inland from Veracruz to Tenochtitlán, for Cortés followed it in 1519. Aztec *pochteca* followed well-trodden paths with their long caravans of human porters, heavily laden with goods, or had their loads transferred to canoes for transport by river and in coastal waters. Aztec garrisons were established at vulnerable points on the trade routes.

CHAPTER FOUR

THE WORLD OF WORK

Opportunities for Mesoamericans were limited by birth. We know this from Spanish records about the Aztecs, their contemporaries and the Maya in the 16th century. Also, because the archaeological record of preceding Mesoamerican cultures is similar to that of the Aztec and Maya and indicates that there was continuous development, we can project the nature of Aztec society back into pre-Aztec times. The top military, legal, administrative and priestly positions were open only to members of the hereditary nobility; among the middle class of skilled artisans and merchants, most were probably glad to follow their family profession, since it could provide sufficient wealth to secure a good level of comfort. Most people had their living from the land, the men working as fishermen, hunters and farmers.

In terms of food and basics, common people could be self-sufficient. They grew most, if not all, of the food they ate. They often had sufficient skills to produce pots, clothing, basketwork and tools for their own use. Some might produce a surplus of cloth or tools that could be bartered for luxury items – a turkey, some meat or extra vegetables, decorated clothing and so on – at market. They were also connected to the wider world of religious life, ceremonial centres and military campaigns through their responsibilities to pay taxes or tribute to their rulers and to serve in the army or as labourers in construction projects when required.

Left: A codex scene depicts the harvesting of cacao. Farming was the principal livelihood of most Mesoamericans.

IN THE STATE'S SERVICE

The administration of the Aztec empire and its largely self-governing constituent units was a major task and provided employment for large numbers or people. All the most important and senior positions were filled by members of the *pipiltin* nobility. Nobles served as advisers to the ruler, as ambassadors, as governors of allied provinces, as judges, as collectors of tax and tribute, as leading members of the military hierarchy and as bureaucrats. Others joined the priesthood, where they had opportunities to pursue intellectual interests in, say, astronomy, mathematics or writing. All these men were graduates of elite *calmecac* priestly schools.

Commoners – whose living came from farming, fishing, hunting, soldiering, artisan work or mercantile activity – could rise to positions of authority within the *capultin* or tribal clans to which they

Below: A painted Maya pot of c.AD600–900, from the Motagua valley, shows a dignitary carrying shield and spear.

belonged. One was elected *calpullec*, who oversaw economic matters, such as grants of land, within the clan; another was the *teochcautin*, the keeper of laws. At times of conflict, the *teochcautin* led the clan's conscripts to war.

THE KING'S MEN

Similarly, in Maya culture commoner-farmers, fishermen and soldiers could not rise to the most senior administrative and economic positions. In the Maya cities of the Classic Period, the top military staff, administrators and traders were all members of the upper nobility. The top military chief, *sahal*, was generally one of the king's closest relatives.

In Postclassic Yucatán, as described by Bishop Diego de Landa, the ruler of a regional state, called the *halach uinic*, appointed those who governed the towns

Above: Clay figurines from Jaina Island show the elaborate headdresses, jewellery and other adornments of the Maya elite.

and villages of the region from the highest levels of royalty and the nobility, including his own nephews, cousins and brothers. Each of these men, who were called *batabs*, ruled through a council of two or three and decisions on regional matters had to be approved unanimously by all councillors.

The *batab* was the local judge and military leader. He ensured that his town or region was ready with its economic tribute when required by the *halach uinic*. The *batab* had two or three deputies called *ah kulelob* to perform his bidding. He worked closely with a military specialist called a *nacom*, a noble who served in this highly prestigious and coveted position for three years. During this period, he was required to live a celibate and sober life, with no contact of any kind with women. Even those who waited upon him and served his food were required to be men.

Another group of senior administrators were the *ah holpopob* who ran the council meeting house and were well informed on matters of foreign interaction. Day-to-day matters such as village disputes or petty crimes were the province of the *tupiles* or local law officers.

COPÁN'S GOVERNORS

Archaeologists working at Copán have uncovered details of civil administrators in the reign of King Yax Pac (AD763–820). Leading nobles, who lived in the region of Copán called Las Sepulturas by historians, were members of Copán's ruling council and each headed a prestigious blood lineage. Their houses have been excavated and contain splendid carved benches that suggest that these men had significant independent authority and wealth.

One of these was the king's chief scribe, Max Chanal, whose house contains several portraits of him holding his tools. A delicately carved bench dedicated in AD781 celebrates his own rank, his proud descent and the might of his king.

Yax Pac's brothers, Yahua Chan and Yax K'amlay, were also important figures in the administration. Scholars believe that the king's authority was failing and that he attempted to bolster it by giving more power to his brothers and to leading nobles. However, the attempt was doomed to failure. After his death, the dynasty and Copán itself suffered the effects of a decline that had already begun some years earlier.

THE QUICHÉ ARISTOCRACY

Among the Quiché Maya of highland Guatemala, once again, commoners were excluded from the highest levels of government and administration. The nobility or *ahauab* were descendants of the Quiché founders, who were probably originally Putún Maya merchants from the Gulf Coast lowlands of Mexico. The *ahauab* provided rulers, military leaders, priests and administrators.

Members of the middle class could find work as land managers, soldiers, traders and bureaucrats. The *ahauab* were organized into groups depending on descent from a common father. Members of particular kin groups specialized in serving as priests, warriors or administrators. The leaders of these kin groups governed their relatives and served as advisers to the Quiché ruler.

At the Quiché capital Utatlan in the 15th century, three lineages were pre-eminent and identified with gods: the Ahau Quiché were followers of the sky god, the Nihaib were dependents of the moon goddess and the Cawek were devotees of the sun god. Their elite members filled the top administrative posts of army captain, judge and other positions identified as 'speaker' and 'receiving officer', a kind of ambassador and master of ceremonies who received important visitors. Above them all was the ahpop ('Ruler or Mat Lord'). He was high priest, army leader and chairman of the ruling council.

Above: A jade chest piece from Nebaj, Guatemala, c.AD300–900, depicts a seated nobleman.

Below: A limestone carving from Palenque shows King Pacal, seated on a regal jaguar-head stool, receiving a headdress – and so divine authority to rule – from his mother Zac Kuk. Archaeologists found the relief inside House E of the Palenque palace.

CHAPTER FIVE

EVERYDAY LIFE

The day started early for Mesoamericans: the people of Tenochtitlán rose before dawn. When the morning star, Venus, appeared in the sky, drums and conch trumpets sounded from the Templo Mayor and the temples that were the focus of religious life in each locality. The *tlatoani*, his relatives and the nobles, priests, farmers, fishermen, hunters and merchants all awoke. Many took a steam bath to refresh themselves. For most, breakfast was a few tortillas or tamales, perhaps a cup of *atolli* or maize soup. Labourers carried a few more maize snacks to work for a midday meal.

In a Maya village or city of the Classic Period, the first hours of the day were markedly similar. The majority rose before dawn, took a steam bath, ate a maize breakfast and made their way to the fields, artisan-workshop or other place of work grasping a few tortillas for later sustenance.

After a long day's labour, most workers were home before dark. They ate their largest meal, again based on maize, at this time. Some accounts suggest that labourers, hungry from their labours in the fields, ate as many as 20 large tortillas at evening meal. Men and women usually ate separately, squatting or sitting on the floor. Afterwards, lighting their homes with pine torches, both men and women often settled down to craft-work, perhaps chipping simple tools from flint or making pots for their own use. Merchants, by contrast, sometimes hosted elaborate feasts, while in noble houses evenings of poetry and music might be laid on in gardens and patio areas giving on to luxuriously appointed dining areas.

Left: A page from the Mixtec Codex Zouche-Nuttall depicts the wedding of Lady 3-Flint to Lord 12-Wind.

LIFE IN THE HOME

In Tenochtitlán, the *tlatoani's* divine magnificence was reflected in the splendour of his elegantly decorated palace, surrounded by gardens containing ponds, walkways, an aviary and even a zoo. Members of the *pipiltin* nobility also had palatial residences with a *temazcalli* or steam bath and expansive gardens, while wealthy merchants and craftsmen expressed their social standing in fine, but much smaller houses. The home of a common family was a single-roomed hut, or a few rooms clustered around a courtyard. Walls were usually of adobe or wattle and daub, although some wealthier commoners lived in stone buildings.

Multiroom houses contained one or more bedrooms, a living room with a central hearth and perhaps a bathroom. Single-room huts provided little more

Below: Aztecs lived on or near the floor, sitting on reed mats to eat and work at weaving or toolmaking close to the hearth.

than a space for sleeping, with the family hearth often situated outside beneath a canopy. The family might keep a turkey or a small dog in a pen alongside the house or a few birds in a cage. Many households also had a small garden called a *xochichinancalli* ('flowerbed among the reeds') for growing vegetables, flowers and healing herbs. All houses had a shrine to the ancestors. The location as well as the size of a family's home depended on their wealth and social standing.

WORKING FROM HOME

Home was a place of labour for women, who spent long hours spinning, weaving and cooking. They span thread from maguey agave, henepen or cotton using a handheld drop spindle, working it into woven cloth using a loom strapped on the back and held in the lap. When not weaving or sewing, they ground maize for hours using a rolling stone or pestle at a low table called a *metatl*. With maize dough they made tortillas on a large clay disc laid over a fire on three hearthstones.

Above: This modern reconstruction of an Aztec working family shows a farmer bringing home crops while his relatives weave and attend to the children.

Poorer families generally lived farther away from the city centre. They often lived in single-room huts, whereas the better off families lived in stone buildings nearer the city's ceremonial precincts and major markets. Aztec houses had little or no furniture: people worked, sat and ate on the floor. They usually slept on woven reed mats.

The men worked in the *chinampa* fields or took their boats, nets and harpoons out fishing on the lake. They taught their sons how to fish and encouraged them to try their luck at catching birds. If the conscription call came, they could be forced to go on military campaign in the army or perhaps to serve as labourers in a vast building construction project designed to express the might and celebrate the religious devotion of the 'people of the sun'.

Left: The kind of thatched hut typically occupied by Maya peasants is depicted amid trees in a detail from a temple mural.

WITHIN THE CORNER POSTS

In the lowlands of the central Maya region, the typical commoner's house was built on a low platform of earth or rubble, with walls of stone, mud blocks or adobe built around four wooden corner posts and a roof of pole and thatch. Sometimes only the lower half of the wall was made of long-lasting materials such as stone or adobe, and the upper part was filled in with straw or reeds. The house contained one or two rooms at most.

Builders often laid out three or four of these small constructions around a central courtyard. According to Bishop Diego de Landa, the Maya of Yucatán split these houses lengthways by building an internal wall. In the rear, private part they built bed frames of branches and saplings over which they laid mats as mattresses. Here they slept, using cloaks as coverings.

The front part of the house functioned as a kind of porch, and provided a cooler place to sleep in hot weather. In some areas a family group might have used several small buildings arranged around a central yard: one for storing food, tools and equipment, one for sleeping, one as a living area, one as a shrine, one as a workshop for making stone tools – and a small hut with a central fire heating stones for use as a steam room. Some Maya villagers stored food and water in pits called *chultunes* dug in the ground.

As among the Aztecs, the majority of men were away from home for long hours working in the fields or hunting. At home, the women worked ceaselessly spinning, weaving, grinding flour, preparing food, tending to the garden and the needs of the turkeys or dogs they kept for meat.

Any cloth that was not needed, together with surplus vegetables or other items that could be spared from the garden were taken to the nearest market to be sold or to barter for items which the family did not make themselves.

At times of sowing and harvest the division of labour shifted, so that women went out to assist their menfolk in the fields with the extra seasonal work.

FAMILY NETWORK

People tended to live in family or extended family groups. At Tikal, an extended family often lived in houses arranged on the north, south and west sides of a courtyard and facing east towards a fourth building on a higher platform. This probably contained a shrine to the ancestors and, beneath the floor, the graves of the most revered among past family members.

All members of Maya settlements lived in the same pattern of buildings. Wealthier members such as nobles, traders, military leaders and the king lived in increasingly splendid versions of the basic buildings.

Below: Carving on an archway in Labná depicts a simple, one-roomed thatched hut.

BEATING THE ODDS

According to Spanish chroniclers, the Aztecs were devoted gamblers. All Mesoamerican games had religious overtones because they saw the entire universe as structured by and charged with divine meaning. Even the apparently chance events of a sporting contest or a gambling pastime were open to interpretation and might provide guidance from the gods.

THE BALL GAME

By far the greatest devotion was reserved for the ball game. It was played in various forms from at least the mid-second millennium BC in Mesoamerica. Two teams of players on an I-shaped earth or stone court tried to send a hard rubber ball through a stone loop set high on one or both walls – or in some versions into the 'end zone' behind their opponents – using elbows, hips and legs. The game was rich in religious symbolism. The ball might be identified with the sun, or the match interpreted as a re-enactment

Above: The test of daring called voladores. *Later, the men will swing upside down around the pole on the end of the ropes.*

of sacred battles between the Aztec gods Quetzalcóatl and Tezcatlipoca or between the Maya Hero Twins and the lords of the underworld. Spectators gambled on the outcome of matches. The game must have been an exhilarating spectacle, played at high speed by very skilled and brave performers wearing elaborate protective costumes. Nevertheless, the ball game was so deeply coloured by its many religious overtones that it was more a religious ceremony than a public sporting contest.

THE BEAN GAME

Another ancient Mesoamerican game of chance and skill, called *patolli* by the Aztecs, was played on the ground using a cross-shaped board of 52 squares painted on a mat or scratched into plaster or clay. Players moved blue and red pieces around the board according to the throw of dice, with the aim of moving all one's pieces to the centre of the cross. The game that developed into *patolli* was played at least as early as the 7th century AD, when a

Left: On the feast of Xocotluetzi, young men competed in climbing the pole to be first to take hold of symbols hanging there.

board was marked out on the floor of the Zacuala residential building in Teotihuacán. About 100–200 years later, no fewer than three boards were marked on the plaster floor of the Palacio Quemado at Tollán.

The cross-shaped Aztec board appears to have been a simplification of an older design incorporating a cruciform shape and squares. *Patolli*, like the ball game, was played throughout Mesoamerica. The Maya marked out playing boards at many ancient sites including Tikal, Uaxactún, Piedras Negras, Chichén Itzá, Palenque and Dzibilchaltún.

In their version of the game, the Aztecs used inscribed kidney beans as their dice – their name *patolli* derives from the Nahuatl word for kidney bean. Both players and onlookers placed wagers: according to a report by Diego Durán, a noisy group would gather around the game and bet on the players. Wealthy merchants and members of the nobility risked large amounts of gold and precious jewels on the outcome; others bet what they could afford. Desperate gamers are said to have bet their house or even their freedom on the result. Durán's report indicated that the game was called *totoloque* and that both playing pieces and dice were made of gold, but scholars believe he must have been mistaken on this last point.

Winning or losing was in the hands of the gods. Durán wrote that players would pray to Macuilxóchitl, god of pleasure and of games, and cast incense into a nearby brazier before making a throw. Sometimes priestly diviners would be asked to interpret the outcome of a throw or of a game. The mat was portable, so the game could be played anywhere, even in the streets. Spanish chroniclers' accounts suggest that *patolli* was played with remarkable and noisy fervour at all hours of night and day in Tenochtitlán.

The Aztecs also played a game resembling checkers on a mat or board marked with squares, using black and white pieces.

POLE GAMES

Two remarkable tests of skill and strength centred on descending or climbing a tall pole. One was a contest associated with the festival of the god Huehuetéotl. Several men competed to be first to reach the top of a very tall pole and grasp an icon of Huehuetéotl that had been placed there.

Another game, dubbed *voladores* ('flyers') by the Spanish conquistadors, involved five men. The five players clambered to the top of a pole. Four attached themselves by one ankle to ropes that were wound elaborately around the pole while the fifth settled himself with flute and drum on a wooden platform at the top of the pole.

As the drummer-flautist played his musical instruments, each of the four flyers leapt headfirst from the pole. Falling upside down, the men would swing round and round by the ankle very fast and getting closer and closer to the ground as the rope unravelled. Just before the flyer smashed his head on the ground, the man would pull himself up on the rope with his hands. This meant that he landed feet-first on the ground – and the momentum then carried him forward at a fast pace. An image from the *Codex Borbonicus* depicts the men circling the pole on ropes to the beat of the drum,

while a priest standing on the steps of a nearby temple pyramid calls down a blessing on the proceedings.

This test of skill as performed by the Aztecs is still attempted in the early 21st century in the Gulf Coast region of Mexico.

Above: Diego Durán gave a full account of patolli *in the* Codex Durán. *This image, from that codex, is of a variant of the game.*

Below: These columns are all that remains of Tollán's Palacio Quemado, where three patolli *boards were marked on the floor.*

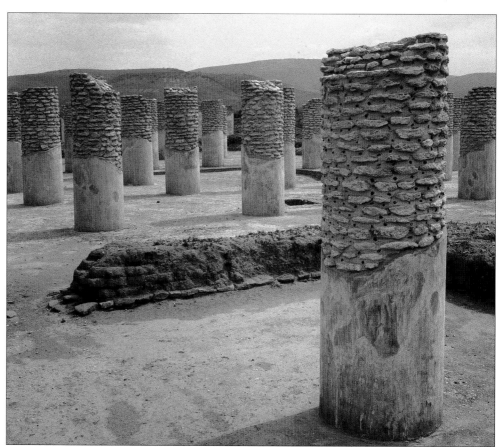

THE BEAT OF THE DRUM

For the Aztecs, music, dancing and singing were among the highest arts. Musicians aspired to be like the great Toltecs of Tollán, masters of every craft and creative art who were celebrated for composing from the very deep places of their hearts and so making music divine. The Aztecs valued dance and music both in profane and sacred contexts, not only as a form of recreation and communal celebration such as in naming ceremonies for children or at marriage feasts, but also as an act of religious devotion, an integral part of ceremonies honouring the gods.

Below: Dressed for ceremonial performance. This carved whistle is from Nebaj, Guatemala, c.AD300–900.

THE SONG HOUSE

Both these forms of music and dance were taught to the young. In the *calmecac* schools of the nobility – where the teachers were priests and where pupils were fledgling rulers, scribes and men of religion – sacred music and ritual dances were taught. In the *telpochcalli* schools frequented by commoners, the future workers of the empire were instructed in love songs, war songs and profane dances. Each of the *telpochcalli* was equipped with a special area called a *cuicalli* ('song house'), consisting of a courtyard surrounded by rooms. The school's highly respected music teacher would place his drums in the centre of the yard and the children would be put through their paces as he played and instructed them in the steps of the dance.

The Spanish churchman Gerónimo de Mendieta, writing in the 16th century, reported that Aztec nobles kept a composer as part of their domestic staff. The composer would write new songs and dances for religious festivals, but also to mark secular events such as a war triumph, a noble wedding or the accession of a new ruler.

DRUMS AND PIPES

Aztec music was stronger on rhythm than on melody: musicians created a strong beat on drums, rattles and rasps. There were two main types of drum: the *huehuetl*, which stood upright, consisted of animal skin stretched over the ends of a carved wooden frame and was played with the hands, while the *teponaxtli*, which was laid horizontally on a circular base, was split to form a double tongue that the drummer hit with rubber-headed hammers to produce a two-tone note. Other musicians complemented the drummers' rhythm with rattles and scrapers made from notched human or animal bone. Wind instruments included conches (large seashells) and flutes, whistles and trumpets (usually made of

Above: This impressivve example of the Aztec huehuetl *('vertical drum') or war drum is carved with warrior imagery.*

clay). Dancers contributed to the music with hand-held gourds filled with seeds, or with anklets of seashells.

The Maya also led their music with rhythm. They had a wide variety of drums. The *tunkul* was, like the Aztec *huehuetl*, an upright drum: the Maya version was made from a hollowed tree trunk and was often as tall as the drummer's chest, with a deerskin stretched over the end. A second Maya drum was identical to the Aztec *teponaxtli*, with two wooden tongues played with hammers, while

Right: Sacred steps in the round. Aztec dancers encircle a minimalist orchestra in this image from the Codex Durán.

another was made from a tortoise shell and played with the palm. Bishop Diego de Landa reported that this tortoise drum gave issue to a very doleful sound. A fourth drum was made from clay and shaped like two vases set base to base, with a membrane at each end. Musicians also played panpipes, conch shells and trumpets of clay or wood. They also had flutes carved from hollowed human leg bones, deer bones and reeds or fashioned from clay. Dancers tied copper, gold or silver bells to their wrists, legs and waist and played a small hand-held drum, called a *pax*, as they danced.

STREET ENTERTAINERS

Music and singing accompanied street entertainments provided by jugglers, acrobats and clowns. Troupes of entertainers laid on dances and comic entertainments for the elite at the courts of rulers and on the spacious patios of noblemen's houses, but also for the commoners in marketplaces, on streets and even outside the cities in small villages. Since trade was performed by barter and currency was little used even at market, they doubtless performed for their supper or for a supply of tortillas, beans and vegetables to take away for later consumption. Hernán Cortés took a troupe of acrobats with him back to Europe, where they performed at the imperial court of Charles V in Spain.

Right: A Mixtec figurine celebrates Macuilxóchitl, patron of the ball game and of the board game patolli, *and god of music.*

FESTIVAL OF THE MUSIC GOD

Macuilxóchitl, who was associated with gambling in his guise as god of pleasure and of games, was also considered to be the patron deity of musicians. He was connected to flower god Xochipilli and to the calendrical day-name '5-flower'.

Macuilxóchitl was sometimes shown with a symbol like a butterfly in place of his mouth. In his role as music god, he might take the form of a turtle. Before his feast day in Tenochtitlán,

devotees fasted then covered themselves with jewellery and symbols of the god. According to Bernardino de Sahagún, the ceremony included songs and dancing to the resonant beat of a drum, before worshippers made offerings of animal blood and specially baked cakes to Macuilxóchitl. At the climax of the feast-day celebration, Sahagún reported, priests put a company of slaves to death to satisfy the music god's thirst.

LYRICS AT THE FEAST

Aztec poets found an enthusiastic audience for their work at elite banquets in the leading cities of the empire. Rulers, princes and nobles shared a love of metaphorical language and lyrical self-expression. Masters of verse and philosophical reflection recited their poems in the patio areas of palaces and noble homes, to the accompaniment of music on flutes and drums, while stars danced overhead in the deep blue of night. Most members of the elite classes, including rulers such as Netzahualcóyotl of Texcoco and Tecayehuatzin of Huexotzingo, were poets.

GENRE POETRY

The verses came in a range of genres. One group, known as *xochicuicatl* ('flower songs'), focused on the pleasures and consolations of nature's beauty for those afflicted by suffering. Another group was

THE POET NEZAHUALCÓYOTL

Nezahualcóyotl, ruler of Texcoco, was celebrated as a warrior, wise king and writer of laws. While his forebears and contemporaries were devoted to many gods, he built a temple to a single deity he called Ipalnemoani ('The One By Which We Live') or Tloquenahuaque ('The One Who is Always Near'). He was also a celebrated and sensitive poet, who often examined the pain humans feel due to the changes brought about by the movement of time – which was called *cahuitl* ('the power that departs from us') in the Nahuatl language.

One of his poems declared: 'What can put down lasting roots in this place of change? Everything here is only passing. Even the most precious creations, of jade and turquoise, end in pieces, crumbling to dust.'

yaocuicatl ('war songs'), which expressed a fierce joy in conflict and traced the movements of the mind and heart in battle. *Xopancuicatl* ('spring songs') celebrated the new life of the fields in spring, reminding listeners of the spirit's quickening when maize shoots return after winter. A fourth type were *icnocuicatl* ('orphan songs'). They described the pleasures of life, while recalling the ephemeral nature of all pleasures. One declared: 'The time will come for us all to go, by day or by night, down into the mysteries of death. Here on earth we have time to know ourselves, briefly we pass over the earth's surface.'

The language of the Aztec poets was rich in metaphor. Their poetry was 'song and flowers' bloom'; when a poet

Left: Xochipilli, god of poetry, flowers and souls, was also a symbol of summer. This image is from the Codex Vaticanus.

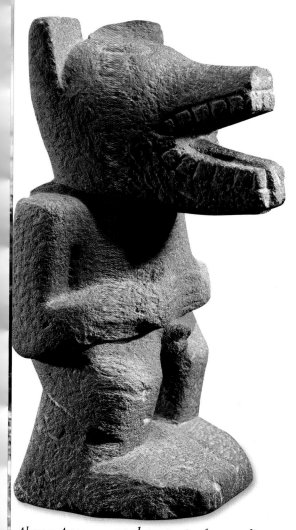

Above: An unusual portrait of a standing coyote, this stone carving was made by a Totonac sculptor and found at Ihuatzio.

stepped forward to speak he entered into the 'flowering space', the 'spring arena' or the 'house of blooms'. He called political and temporal power 'the place on the mat'.

Tenochtitlán was 'eagle and cactus place' because the México/Aztecs had traditionally founded the city at the spot where they saw an eagle on a cactus, in fulfilment of their god Huitzilopochtli's promise. The city was also 'home of white willows' in reference to the trees that grew there and 'place of darts' because of weapon production in the city.

Poets celebrated warfare as 'shield and dart', 'a singing of shields', and as 'the place where the shields' mist clears'. Poets often spoke of self-knowledge in terms of 'knowing his face'. In Mesoamerican philosophy, the face was seen as the place in which the self resided. Aztec poets could find employment within the religious establishment, as composers of the many hymns – in honour of gods such as Huitzilopochtli, Centéotl, and Tláloc – sung as part of the great religious ceremonies. They also wrote epic poetry, for example the narratives of the birth of the god Huitzilopochtli, of the creation of the world and succession of five world eras, of the many gifts to humankind and the heroic actions of the god-prince Quetzalcóatl.

PUBLIC DEBATE

Another body of literary figures, who may also have been poets, were the *tlamatinime* ('the Ones who Know'). They produced prose works called *huehuehtlahtolli* ('statements of ancient knowledge') that contained philosophical questions, along with statements about duty, death and honour. Sometimes these works were read and debated in public ceremonies. One takes the form of an address by a father to his daughter, in which he warns his offspring that the world is a place of suffering, exhaustion and disappointment, of pain caused by burning sun and winds sharp as obsidian blades. However, he adds that the bitter taste of life is sweetened by compensations such as sensory pleasure, laughter, physical strength and bravery.

A VOICE AT COURT

We have little evidence of the role of Maya scribes in producing poetry and secular writing other than official documents such as the tribute lists, marriage papers or the genealogical histories. However, we know from reports by Diego de Landa and other post-Conquest sources that the Maya enjoyed communal celebrations involving both sacred hymns and secular music with dancing.

The revered *ah ts'ib* or *ah k'u'hun* of Classic Period Maya cities, who proudly wore his pens in his long hair as a status symbol and badge of office, was celebrated for his facility both with language and with images. This exalted figure sat with rulers and their intimates at great state occasions and must surely have given right expression to the feelings of the group in songs and poems. A people that so appreciated the visual arts and music are likely to have been an appreciative audience for the skilful use of words.

Below: This chocolate goblet is decorated with an image of a Maya prince enjoying the drink.

115

THE HEALING ARTS

To the Aztecs healing was sacred: their main word for doctor, *teopati*, combined *patli* ('medical arts') and *teo* ('holy'). Aztec creation narrative explained the cause of sickness. At the start of the fifth or current world age, the existing race of humankind was made from the bones of the men and women who had lived in the fourth world age. These bones had been languishing in the underworld, but the Feathered Serpent god Quetzalcóatl ventured into that dark realm to rescue them. However, the Feathered Serpent was tricked during his escape from the underworld and dropped the bones, which broke into many pieces. He carried the remains to the home of the gods, where all the divine lords and ladies agreed that the bones should be ground to a powder, then moistened with the gods' blood and mixed to a paste. From this paste the first people of the fifth world age were made. People suffered illness, old age and death because they were originally made from broken bones. However, they had a special calling to serve the gods because they were fashioned from the gods' blood.

THREE SPIRIT CENTRES

People were made according to the same divine template that structured all parts of the universe. Just as the universe had a tripartite structure – with the heavens above, the terrestrial plane in the middle and the underworld beneath – so three spirit centres existed within the human body. The first, residing in the head, was *tonalli* ('hotness'). This was the counterpart of the soaring heavens.

When a body lost *tonalli*, death followed – and so a corpse was cold. People dissipated *tonalli* by self-indulgence in sex or drunkenness. They could boost it by bravery in battle and by living an austere, self-restrained life. Doctors sometimes prescribed herbal fragrances to increase a patient's *tonalli*. In the natural way of things, *tonalli* increased with age and old people were respected for having a strong *tonalli*. When a shaman or diviner embarked on a spirit voyage, it was his *tonalli* that left his body and entered another realm.

The second spirit centre, *teyolia*, was the counterpart of the terrestrial plane and was situated in the heart. *Teyolia* was the source of our thoughts, creative impulses and human personality. Tenochtitlán's noble poets were rich in the quality of *teyolia*. This, too, was weakened by sensual indulgence. The *teyolia* was akin to the Western idea of the soul in that it departed the body at death and travelled to its fate in the afterlife – the underworld for most, but one of the levels of heaven for those who had been sacrificed, killed in battle, died giving birth or suffered various watery deaths associated with the rain god Tláloc.

The third spirit centre, *ihiyotl*, situated in the liver, was the counterpart of the underworld. Energy, life's breath and

Left: The Florentine Codex *(1575–77) depicts various Aztec medical procedures, including a cure for haemorrhoids, treating a fever and the binding of a broken leg.*

passionate desire were the products of *ihiyotl*. Lazy people, who lacked drive and the power to achieve things, were understood to have a badly functioning *ihiyotl*.

A HEALTHY BALANCE

The three parts of the universe were perpetually held in balance by natural order, by the four cardinal directions and by the tree of life that majestically rose in the centre of the universe connecting heaven, earth and underworld. Doctors taught that the way to health lay in safeguarding the good functioning of the three spirit centres of the body and ensuring a natural balance between them. An unexpected reverse or accident might damage one of the centres and cause illness or disturbed behaviour. For example, a shock resulting in emotional turmoil would be expected to damage a person's *ihiyotl*.

SPIRITUAL HEALING

Throughout Mesoamerica healing combined knowledge of herbal remedies with trust in the power of shamans and diviners to seek and remedy the causes of health problems. In addition, all peoples of Mesoamerica put faith in the power of public bloodletting and sacred ritual to

satisfy the gods and avert disease, famine, earthquake and other natural disasters. Physical and spiritual were intertwined: illnesses or disturbances might have physical or spiritual causes and could be treated with spiritual or physical means, or both. A doctor might tell a woman with a severe cold that she had suffered damage to her *tonalli*. He could use his knowledge of herbal medicine to prescribe a fragrance to boost her *tonalli*. Equally, he might seek out the spiritual cause of the malaise by sending her to a diviner.

Above: A Mixtec codex celebrates the god of medicine. Aztecs revered Patécatl, who was also god of drunkenness, as lord of medicine.

The diviner would seek to discover whether the damage to the woman's *tonalli* was caused by a curse from one of the gods. Sometimes the diviner might take hallucinogenic mushrooms, peyote or morning glory seeds to bring on a trance in which he could discover the cause and find a way to appease the god in question. He might throw coral seeds and seek answers from the movement of sensations in his body.

Aztec doctors were divided broadly into those treating physical symptoms, the *teopati*, and those seeking and addressing spiritual causes, *tictli*, men who could read the divine patterns and structures of the universe. The medical specialists were expert in herbal medicine, the *tlametpatli*, who drew on their ancient healing art to treat problems including heart trouble, stomach sickness and breathing disorders. In markets across the empire, *panamacanis* sold mixed herbal remedies.

Left: A detail from the Florentine Codex *shows a plant used to treat fever. Healers administered bitter medicines wrapped in chocolate paste to patients.*

SACRED THEATRE

Large-scale public sacrifices on the steps of temple pyramids made a powerful statement of secular power as well as of religious devotion. In Tenochtitlán, visiting dignitaries witnessed an overwhelming proof of the city's great power, which was sufficient to build the vast sacred arena, mobilize a cadre of magnificently attired priests and musicians and bring to sacrifice a vast army of prisoners.

RITES OF SACRIFICE

The crowds which gathered for the ceremony celebrated the power of the gods who demanded and were worthy of such ritual; the glory of the ruler who could command such a display; and – a central

RITUAL SONGS

The Aztecs sang hymns to honour their gods during religious ceremonies. Sacred songs have survived to the goggle-eyed rain god Tláloc, to flower god Xochipilli, to strong-limbed maize deities Chicomecóatl and Centéotl and to the war lord Huitzilopochtli. The hymn in praise of Xochipilli declares that the sacred quetzal bird sings its joy in the flower lord during the dark hours of midnight, while the worshipper makes his song at dawn, adding that praise will rise to Xochipilli from Tláloc's temple.

Tláloc's hymn praises the god as a magician and envisages ancestors at rest or playing at ball in the misty paradise of Tlálocan. Huitzilopochtli's hymn celebrates him as the sun god, who lives among the clouds and the cold air, who as he spreads the brilliance of light stirs a passion for war in the hearts of men. The song, which was probably declaimed by two singers in a stirring answer and response, hails Huitzilopochtli as the instigator of sacred conflicts that result in the defeat and capture of many prisoners for holy sacrifice.

Above: At Chichén Itzá the Temple of the Feathered Serpent – viewed here from the top of the Temple of the Warriors – was an awe-inspiring setting for sacred ritual.

mystery of their religion – the fact that life was dependent on sacrifice. Just as, in Aztec belief, the gods had sacrificed their blood to the creation of humans in the current age and then again to set the sun moving in the sky, so human blood was a necessary offering to maintain sacred order and balance in the cosmos.

Public rites of sacrifice brought the gods to visible life on the temple steps or in sacred processional. A priest or ruler dressed as the god or goddess honoured became that divine form. A priestess wearing a jade skirt was Chalchiúhtlicue in Tenochtitlán, while a Maya ruler might embody the maize god or Chac, lord of rains. Equally, victims destined for sacrifice were considered by the Aztecs to be *ixiptla* ('in the gods' image'). They were believed to contain within their frail human bodies the awesome power of creation and destruction that belonged to the gods,

Right: A detail from the Codex Mendoza *(c.1541) shows part of a sacred ritual as a priest plays drums and sings hymns.*

making possible the re-enactment of the primal scenes of divine sacrifice through which this world's sun and people were brought into being.

The Toltecs and their followers in Tenochtitlán and Chichén Itzá greatly escalated the use of ritual slaughter in religious ceremonies. From the era of Tollán onwards, human sacrifice had a much greater role.

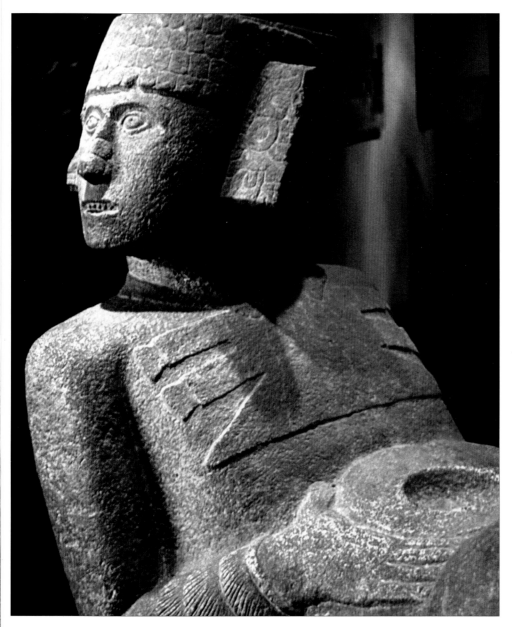

particular musical ceremonies in which they specialized. De Landa described one dance in which two men led the steps. One hurled reeds at the other, who exhibited great skill in catching them, all the while following the steps of the dance. Another dance witnessed by de Landa was a sacred war dance, in which as many as 800 men carrying small banners followed a complex pattern of steps in perfect unison. In Tenochtitlán, the leading warriors, priests and members of the *pipiltin* nobility engaged in a sacred dance with their divine ruler at the climax of enthronement ceremonies that began the rule of a new *tlatoani*.

Below: In the gods' image. A Maya funerary urn, c.AD250–900, represents a fearsome-looking priest dressed in ritual costume.

Above: Offering plate. A chacmool from Tenochtitlán holds the hollowed dish used to display the hearts of sacrificial victims.

INCENSE AND DANCING

Ceremonies were accompanied by the burning of incense, usually copal resin, but also the resin of the rubber and chicle trees. Worshippers believed that as the smoke rose it became food for the gods and goddesses. In sacrifices to placate the rain god, his human petitioners told that the clouds of incense had the power to attract the dark, rain-heavy clouds for which they prayed. Before burning, cakes of resin were painted turquoise blue, the colour of sacrifice. When worshippers could not provide a jaguar or alligator for animal sacrifice, the incense was sometimes moulded into the shape of an animal heart. In the Cenote of Sacrifice at Chichén Itzá, a worshipper made an offering of an incense ball containing a cake of vegetable material in the shape of a human heart.

Music played an important role in the theatre of the sacred. Large bands of musicians took part in sacred processions and sacrificial ceremonies, playing clay and shell trumpets, drums and rattles, and creating a mournful howl with conch shells. The celebrated murals at Bonampak represented a 12-man orchestra as part of a procession: they played tortoise-shell drums, ceramic trumpets and seed-filled gourds.

Among the Maya, group dances were very serious and highly sacred. According to Bishop Diego de Landa, groups of men and women danced separately and had

WHERE THE ANCESTORS GO

The Aztecs were taught not to fear death. Life and death were one aspect of the sacred duality that structured the universe, a duality also expressed in oppositions such as day and night, hot and cold, light and darkness.. Life was not easy, suffering was inevitable and death was inescapable. Many deaths were celebrated as honourable, for example, dying in giving birth, in battle or in a rite of human sacrifice. For the Aztecs it was a matter of honour to embrace death with equanimity and with a certain pride.

DAY OF THE DEAD

The Aztecs' positive attitude to death has carried through into modern Mexican celebrations on the Day of the Dead.

The Day of the Dead is celebrated on the Roman Catholic Church feasts of All Saints' Day (1 November) and All Souls' Day (2 November). The first day is usually set aside to remember those who died in childhood and infancy, with departed adults celebrated on the second day.

At home people build small altars in memory of the dead and load them with food, drinks, cakes and sweets – including sweet rolls called *pan de muerto* ('death bread') adorned with dough pieces shaped like bones, and breads called *anima* ('souls'), as well as a cup of the traditional maize soup (*atole*) and for adults beer, tequila and cigarettes. The altars are lit by candles and perfumed with traditional copal incense. The dead are expected to return to share once again in the sensual joys of life on earth. At the family burial plot, relatives gather to hold celebrations including dancing, singing and feasting at the graves of their departed. These festivities are complemented by an open-air Roman Catholic mass.

FLOWERS BLOOM

Each year the people of Tenochtitlán held the festival of Tlaxochimaco ('Coming Forth of Flowers') in honour of ancestors and, in particular, in celebration of the lives of those who had died in the last year. In the first days of the festival, the people gathered wild flowers in the fields near the city and carried them to the temple as an offering to the ancestral tribal god Huitzilopochtli and to Tezcatlipoca, one of the gods of death. They performed ritual dances in memory of the deceased.

The Maya, by contrast, were profoundly fearful of death despite the fact that it was as frequent a visitor among them as it was among the Aztecs. Far from celebrating those who had departed the earth, the bereaved made great demonstrations of their grief with wails of despair by night and floods of tears by day.

Funerary customs also varied among the cultures of Mesoamerica. The ancient way, which was followed widely in the

Above: These figures are part of a procession of gods and goddesses painted on the walls of a noble burial chamber (Tomb 105) in Monte Albán, probably in c.AD500–750.

Below: A skull decorated with shell and jade was laid in the tomb of an Aztec noble who went fearlessly to the spirit world.

settlements of Oaxaca, in Teotihuacán, in Veracruz and throughout Maya regions, was to bury the body in a shroud with a funerary mask for the wealthy and a range of offerings connected to the person's livelihood when alive. The Toltecs and their followers in the Postclassic Period, including the Aztecs, preferred cremation. The body was wrapped in bandages and tied in an upright, seated position before being burned; the resulting ashes were then buried with funerary offerings. Some members of the Aztec elite, however, were granted burial.

RICH AND POOR BURIALS

The burials of rulers, nobles and the wealthy were considerably richer than those of commoners. Elite graves in Classic-Period Maya cities were rich in offerings of jade and serpentine, in funerary masks, jewels and splendid clothes.

In some special cases a pyramid-temple might be erected or an existing structure refashioned to encompass a tomb for the deceased king. A high-ranking scribe would be buried with the pens and other equipment he used to ply his elite trade.

Commoners were generally buried beneath the floor of their houses. In time, as relatives died and were buried

alongside them, the house would be abandoned and used as a family shrine. According to Bishop Diego de Landa, a commoner in Yucatán would be buried in his cotton robe with a few grains of maize or jade beads in his mouth. These would sustain or support him on his voyage along the white road of the Milky Way to the underworld.

Above: Zapotec nobles were buried. Urns such as this one, found in Tomb 113 in Monte Albán, were not used to contain ashes and must have had a ceremonial use.

SACRIFICED IN DEATH

From the 10th century on, the Mixtecs broke open the graves of Monte Albán's former Zapotec rulers and used them to bury their own elite. They left magnificent grave offerings in gold and silver. Slaves and dogs were killed and interred to mark the rank of their former master.

Sacrificial burial appears to have been a Mesoamerican practice as far back as the time of Teotihuacán. A series of burials beneath the Pyramid of the Feathered Serpent contain 137 bodies with hands tied behind the back. Scholars believe they were killed as an offering to the gods upon the completion of the pyramid c.200AD.

Left: The snake, a complex symbol of new life and of the earth, is depicted consuming a human skeleton in a carving from Tula.

PART TWO

ART AND ARCHITECTURE

A carved bone found in the tomb of King Ah Cacau (*r.* AD682–734) beneath Temple I at Tikal depicts the hand of an artist-scribe emerging from a gaping monster's mouth. This monster-mouth was an established Mesoamerican image for the entrance to the spirit realm of the underworld – and the carving indicates that the Maya believed artistic ability and inspiration to have a divine source. Certainly the Maya of the Late Classic Period, in which this bone and the great majority of delicately painted polychrome vases were produced, celebrated their artists as a gifted elite. These exquisite vases – some of the finest produced in any world culture – were often signed by the artists who painted them.

The México/Aztecs, too, revered their artists, whom they called 'Toltecs' after the founders of the city of Tollán/Tula. In the Aztec Nahuatl tongue *tolteca* meant 'artist', and the word for artistic ability was *toltecayotl*. In the years of the Aztec empire, there was no distinction between artists and craftsmen: *tolteca* included artisans such as carpenters and weavers. They were seen as divinely blessed: their task was to seek sacred meaning in their heart and express this truth in their work. If they worked in this way, they would truly be like the Toltecs, whose city of Tollán was remembered as place of beauty and artistic excellence.

This survey of arts and crafts begins with a discussion of the main styles of architecture and a survey of the great cities. It describes the work of potters, weavers and featherworkers, then looks at stone and wood carving, metalwork, jewellery-making, mural painting and the production of painted codex screenfold books. It ends with a discussion of Mesoamerican aesthetics.

Temple I or Great Jaguar Temple, from the terrace of the northern acropolis of the Maya city of Tikal, was once painted red and adorned with moulded plaster masks.

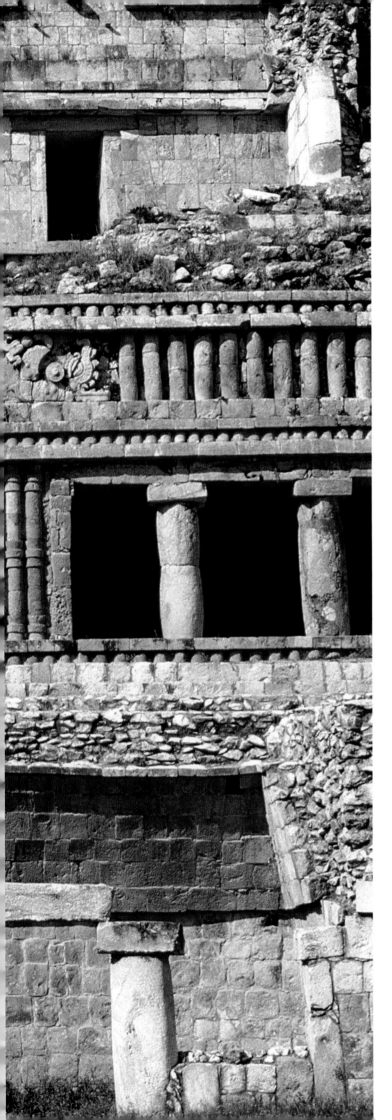

CHAPTER SEVEN

PALACES, TEMPLES AND SACRED CENTRES

Archaeologists generally distinguish between two types of Mesoamerican public building: 'palaces' and 'temples'. Palaces are usually long, low residential and administrative buildings that contain many rooms, small windows, niches above doorways and carved benches. Temples are usually built on top of tall stepped pyramid-platforms, with very limited interior space, and are topped with tall roof combs masonry structures that support a decorative facade. Scholars see palaces as utilitarian, and temples as sacred spaces reserved for ritual activity.

The distinction is helpful, but must be used with some caution since these words are only labels applied retrospectively by historians. Many palaces were used for administrative functions – such as meetings of council groups, or collection and storage of tribute – in addition to being the residences of kings or leading nobles. They contained shrine rooms and areas used for religious ritual such as autosacrifice – the letting of one's own blood. 'Temples', meanwhile, were used for varied purposes in different places and at different times. Some buildings, such as the five-storey palace in Edzná or the Great Palace of Sayil, appear to have combined sacred and utilitarian functions.

Left: In the middle of the three levels of the Palace at Sayil, a pair of columns divides each of the wide chamber doorways.

BUILDING STYLES:
FROM TEOTIHUACÁN TO TIKAL

The architectural style of Teotihuacán was widely influential across Mesoamerica for many hundreds of years. In particular, the city was known for its *talud-tablero* construction, which alternated an upright rectangular section (*tablero*) with a sloping section (*talud*). The *tablero* had a recessed central part.

In Teotihuacán, the style was particularly developed in the Ciudadela or Citadel area of the city, which included the Temple of Quetzalcóatl and 15 other stepped pyramids, as well as two elite residential buildings and an 11-hectare (4.4-acre) open plaza. The Teotihuacános used *talud-tablero* construction only for sacred buildings. At Teotihuacán, the upright *tablero* was always larger than the sloping *talud*, but elsewhere these ratios varied.

Archaeologists do not know for sure where the style originated, although some

Below: Architectural styles such as 'Puuc', 'Chenes' and 'Usumacinta' take their names from the regions in which they developed. This map also shows the main mining areas for certain raw materials.

suggest that immigrants to Teotihuacán from Tlaxcala might have brought a taste for and expertise in this type of building with them. Tlaxcalans, who also brought agricultural expertise in cutting terraced fields and irrigation with dams and canals, were using a form of *talud-tablero* construction in their civic and ceremonial buildings before 300BC, well in advance of the first major sacred buildings at Teotihuacán.

VARIATIONS ON A STYLE

The *talud-tablero* style was used very widely. At Kaminaljuyú *c.*AD200–400 builders either from or influenced by Teotihuacán built a ceremonial centre using *talud-tablero* construction. The style was also used in the Lost World complex at Tikal. At Xochicalco the Temple of the Feathered Serpent played a unique variation on the style by reducing it to the single component of the design: in profile, the temple presents one large sloping *talud* topped with a single *tablero*. Another variation on *talud-tablero* was developed by the builders of the Pyramid of the Niches at El Tajín in Veracruz:

Above: The archway at Kabah, Yucatán, is a good example of the corbelled vault or 'false arch' which looks like an inverted V.

there are six *talud-tablero* levels, with each sloping *talud* topped with a vertical *tablero* containing several niches, and at the top of each *tablero* there is an additional 'flying' reverse *talud*. At Tollán the El Corral temple consisted of two *talud-tablero* levels. The style was revived in the Temple of the Feathered Serpent at Chichén Itzá, which has nine *talud-tablero* tiers. The Aztecs built two small *talud-tablero* buildings in their sacred precinct at Tenochtitlán as an explicit tribute to the sacred city of Teotihuacán.

RAISING THE TEMPLE PLATFORM

In Maya lands builders usually constructed pyramid-platforms from earth and rubble and faced them with cut stone. These platforms usually had four faces with either one stairway or four stairways, one on each face, providing access to the temple on the summit. In some sites, several buildings were built on a single platform, in which case archaeologists usually call the platform an 'acropolis'. The platforms rose from generation to generation, for it was customary to build new platforms and temples over and enclosing the existing sacred structures. The roofs of Maya temples were typically decorated with tall facades of stucco

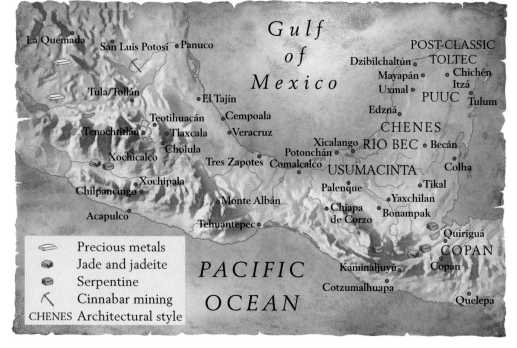

La Quemada
San Luis Potosí • Panuco

Gulf of Mexico

POST-CLASSIC
Dzibilchaltún • TOLTEC
Mayapán • Chichén
Uxmal • Itzá
PUUC • Tulum
Edzná •
CHENES
Xicalango RÍO BEC • Becán
Potonchán •
Comalcalco
USUMACINTA • Colha
Palenque • Tikal
Yaxchilan
Chiapa Bonampak
de Corzo
Quiriguá
COPAN

Tula/Tollán

Teotihuacán • Cempoala
Tenochtitlán • Tlaxcala • Veracruz
Cholula
Xochicalco
El Tajín
Xochipala
Chilpancingo •
Monte Albán
Acapulco
Tres Zapotes
Tehuantepec •

PACIFIC
OCEAN

Kaminaljuyú • Copán
Cotzumalhuapa
Quelepa

Precious metals
Jade and jadeite
Serpentine
Cinnabar mining
CHENES Architectural style

Right: The sloping talud *alternates with the perpendicular* tablero *in the* talud-tablero *construction style perfected at Teotihuacán.*

moulding or mosaic sculpture, usually supported from behind by masonry structures called roof combs. In the mortuary temples of Tikal, the roof comb element contained a portrait of the king buried in a vault beneath the temple platform.

Maya builders of the Classic Period generally relied on the corbelled vault – called the 'false arch' by architectural historians – to support the roof. This structure, which resembles an upside-down V, is created by laying inward-projecting blocks on top of one another: the blocks successively narrow the gap between walls until a single stone can bridge the gap at the top of the arch. (This contrasts with a true arch, whose use was never developed by the Maya, in which the keystone at the top anchors the other stones and creates a structurally much stronger unit.) Corbelled vaults need the support of thick walls beneath them. Maya buildings with false arches had severely reduced interior space given their outer size. Walls were generally made of rubble covered with stone.

BUILDING STYLES

A number of regional styles developed in Maya lands. The sacred buildings of Tikal epitomize the central Petén style, which is characterized by vertiginous pyramid-platforms each topped by a temple with a tall masonry roof comb, a single doorway and thick rubble-filled walls.

At Palenque, Yaxchilán, Piedras Negras and Bonampak the Usumacinta style was characterized by buildings with thinner walls and three or more doorways. At Palenque, for example, builders could erect thinner walls with several doorways

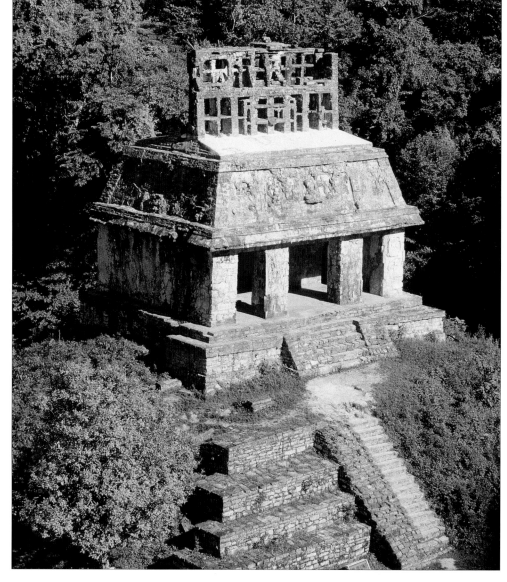

Above: Stucco carving on vertical temple-top roof combs was used to convey dynastic information, as here at Palenque.

because they had replaced the tall vertical facades used in the Petén style with inward-sloping facades that were partly supported by the vaulting of the roof. They also made lighter latticework roof combs rather than the solid masonry ones of the Petén region. Within, the buildings often had two parallel rooms divided by a wall that also helped to bear the roof's weight. A benefit of using thinner walls was that the buildings were considerably lighter and more airy within.

Another regional style of monumental architecture developed at Copán and Quiriguá, where temples, palaces and platforms were decorated with elaborate stucco modelling. A distinctive feature was the building of 'reviewing stands',

which were large platforms with wide access stairways. In the reign of King 18-Rabbit (AD695–738)at Copán, artisans began to create carved stone decorative elements in place of stucco; these were generally painted over with plaster.

Below: From the time of the Toltecs onwards, chacmool *sacrificial figures were placed outside pyramid-top temple sanctuaries.*

A LOVE OF DECORATION: YUCATÁN

The ornate modelling and façades at Copán had counterparts in styles developed farther north in the Maya region. In the Río Bec style, used in the southern Yucatán peninsula in the late Classic Period, builders put decoration and style before function. They erected vast constructions that were essentially reverent imitations of the great pyramids at sites such as Tikal: lofty towers with non-functional steps, doorways that led nowhere and 'false temples' built of solid rock for appearance only. Their buildings had elaborate façades incorporating mosaic masks, which often featured a long-snouted deity believed to be the rain god Chac.

Examples of the style are found at Becán, Xpuhil and Río Bec, in the region north of Calakmul. For example, the building known to archaeologists as Structure 1 at Xpuhil has towers supporting solid temple-like structures with roof combs. Buildings with the appearance of monumental sacred architecture clearly brought prestige to settlements such as Xpuhil or Becán, even if the temples and pyramids could not be used.

The related Chenes style took decorative elements a stage further, creating building façades dominated by decorative masks. In some of these, the entire façade represented a divine face with the doorway as the god's mouth. Chenes-style buildings were raised in the late Classic Period at sites slightly farther north in the

Yucatán peninsula. On the building known as Structure II at Chicanná, the façade represents the face of a god; perhaps the primordial creator Itzamná. The doorway is a serpent mouth, with two stylized eyes and fang-like projections above the opening. The structure gave its name to the settlement, for Chicanná means 'house of the snake's mouth'.

PUUC ELEGANCE

Further north again, the Puuc style developed in the Puuc region in north-western Yucatán. Builders preferred to limit decoration to the upper façade and to keep the lower half of walls plain. They built walls of lime concrete and faced the lower part with limestone veneer. Craftsmen applied pre-cut decorative elements to the upper façades in a repetitive pattern, whose elements were sometimes divine masks or serpents, but were more often abstract patterns such as lattices, fretwork and columns. In developing this style, which appeared at the close of the Classic Period (*c*.AD800–1000), Puuc

Left: The Temple of the Magician, Uxmal, rises to an imposing height against the night sky. Its western stairway climbs to a sanctuary whose entrance is a god's mask.

Above: Intricate decorative patterns and masks of the Maya rain god Chac on the upper walls of the Nunnery Quadrangle at Uxmal are typical of the Puuc style.

builders may been influenced by the repetitive decorative patterns used by their counterparts at Mitla and other sites in Oaxaca.

Splendid examples of the Puuc style are found at Uxmal in the Governor's Palace and the buildings of the Nunnery

---

'THE MAYA REVIVAL'
The US architect Frank Lloyd Wright was greatly impressed with the elegance of Puuc structures and applied the style in several public buildings erected in the 1920s. These created a vogue for a Maya Revival movement in architecture that encompassed other architects including Robert Stacy-Judd, Alfred Bossom and Richard Requa. Stacy-Judd used Maya inspiration in building the ironically named Aztec Hotel in Monrovia, California, in 1924–25. Requa's Maya Revival buildings included the Federal Building in San Diego (1935).

Quadrangle, both of which combine a plain lower wall with intricate decorative designs in the upper façade. The city of Uxmal demonstrates that these architectural styles developed alongside one another and were not mutually exclusive, for the shrine on the first terrace of the Temple of the Magician, at the top of a steep west-side storey, presents its west-facing entrance as the mouth of a divine mask in pure Chenes style.

At Kabáh, which was connected to Uxmal by an 18km (11-mile) *sacbé* causeway, the Temple of the Masks uses masks of the rain god Chac as the repetitive element on the façade. The building is identified as Puuc style by archaeologists, although its façade is entirely covered

Below: The Castillo and Group of the Thousand Columns typified the Chichén Itzá style copied in later Yucatán cities.

with the pattern of masks and so does not feature the plain lower half and decorated upper half typical of pure Puuc. The Great Palace at Sayil and the Palace Arch at Labná are other fine examples of the Puuc style.

TOLTEC ARCHITECTURE
At Chichén Itzá, archaeologists identify two main groups of buildings, with largely distinct styles. The southern group – which includes the Nunnery buildings, the Akabdzib, the House of the Deer, the Red House and the celebrated circular Caracol – is built largely in the Puuc style. The northern group – which includes the Temple of the Warriors, the Group of the Thousand Columns and the great Castillo or Temple of the Feathered Serpent – pioneered a new architectural style in the Maya region, featuring buildings with colonnades. The style exhibited a strong

Above: Sacred entrance. The creator god's face – with fangs and eyes above the door – sanctifies Structure II at Chicanná.

influence from the monumental architecture of sites such as Tollán (Tula) in highland Mexico.

This style became the prototype for building in the Postclassic Period that followed the collapse of Chichén Itzá. The Chichén Itzá style was influential, for example, in the construction of building at Mayapán and Tulum, although the 'copies' were of much poorer quality than the magnificent originals at Chichén Itzá.

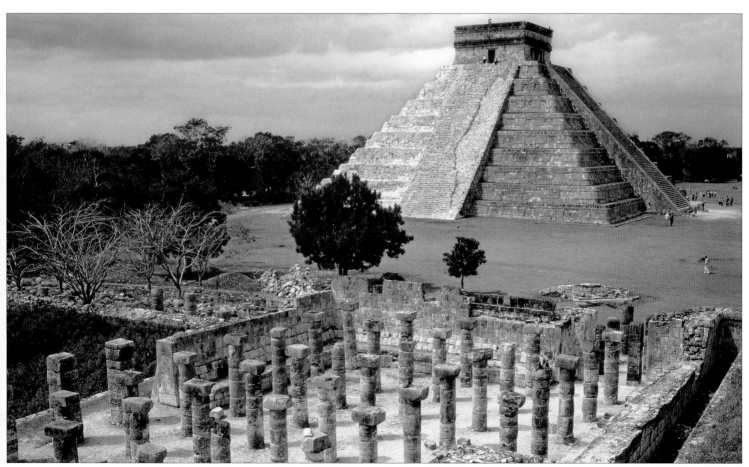

HIDDEN MEANINGS IN SACRED BUILDINGS

At the heart of Tenochtitlán, the Aztecs built up the Templo Mayor over many years on the same sacred site, each new pyramid-temple encompassing its forerunner. The first temple on the site was raised as early as the city's foundation *c.*1325, while improvements and enlargements continued until 1502. This was in line with hallowed Mesoamerican building practice. The great Pyramid of the Sun at Teotihuacán was built in the 1st–2nd centuries AD over a sacred underground cavern and a ground-level shrine, while builders at Tikal, Uaxactún, Chichén Itzá and countless other ceremonial centres followed the same custom, raising their ceremonial structures ever higher, like great mountains, as they built over and on the temples of their ancestors.

In Tenochtitlán, the Aztecs identified the Templo Mayor as a recreation of the holy mountain of Coatépetl on which their tribal god Huitzilopochtli was born. In a number of Maya cities, also, temples were explicitly identified as holy mountains. Stucco masks representing mountains (called *witz*) often flanked the stairways on these structures. Just as a cave in a mountainside was a point of access to the spirit world, so the temple entrance high on a sacred mountain gave access to the supernatural regions.

SACRED TEMPLATE

In Tikal and other cities, architects of ceremonial centres followed a template based on the four cardinal points and three levels of the universe: earth, heaven and underworld. While north was associated with the celestial realm, south was the way to the underworld. East was the place of the rising sun and west, the place of its descent into darkness, represented the earthly realm, governed by time cycles such as the daily pattern of the sun's rising and setting. Buildings in east, west and north were often placed to form a triangle, with the fourth, southern position in the sacred pattern implied.

The scholar Clemency Coggins showed how at Tikal the Twin-Pyramid groups erected to celebrate the end of a *katun*

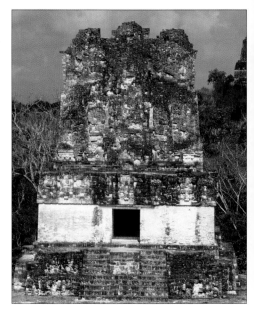

Above: Holy mountain top. Rising 42m (138ft) above the forest floor, Tikal's Temple II outreaches even the towering treetops.

(7,200-day period) were laid out according to this template. These groups consisted of pyramids with four stairways at east and west, with a building containing nine doors lying to the south and a roofless enclosure containing a stela and 'altar' or 'throne' to the north. While the east and west pyramids celebrated the sun's daily cycle, the nine-door southern building represented the underworld, which had nine levels. The northern building was uncovered and so gave access to the sky, the celestial realm of the ancestors. In this place, as if connected to and blessed by his dynastic forebears, the king stood – represented by the stela that named him and the throne stone that celebrated his power.

HOLY NUMBERS

The numerical patterning of Mesoamerican cosmology was regularly celebrated in architecture. Just as the southern

Left: Worshippers gather in the plaza for a katun-ending ceremony at one of the Twin-Pyramid Groups in Tikal.

Right: Copán's G
dedicated in 18-R
linked the Great
palaces and temp

Monte Albán a
are unclear of th
the ball game cl
eras and locati
and in other cc
Period, the ob
been to score
ball through t
other courts, pl
points by making
opponents' endz

Below: The Great
Itzá, seen here fron
overlooked by the

building of the Twin-Pyramid groups at Tikal contained nine doors to represent the nine layers of the underworld, so the 50m (164ft) Temple I at the same site had nine levels. So did the 30m (98ft) Temple of the Feathered Serpent at Chichén Itzá.

The numbers of 365-day and 260-day calendars similarly gave sacred meaning to ceremonial buildings: the Temple of the Niches at El Tajín in Veracruz had 365 niches, while the four staircases of Chichén Itzá's Temple of the Feathered Serpent each contained 91 steps which, when added to the single continuous step at the base, made 365. The Temple of the Masks at Kabah had 260 masks.

RITUAL FURNITURE

In Tollán, Chichén Itzá and Tenochtitlán, adaptations of sacrificial ritual called for specialized pieces of sacred furniture. One was the *chacmool*, carved in the form a reclining figure thought to represent the god Tláloc, with a receptacle on his chest into which a sacrificial victim's heart could be deposited. Another was the skull rack on which the heads of decapitated victims were displayed. These pieces of ritual furniture were used, and might indeed have been invented, by people in

Above: In Frederick Catherwood's engraving Chichén Itzá's Temple of the Feathered Serpent is notable mainly for its mountain-like bulk. But archaeological clearing revealed its intricate design, with 365 steps to match the days of the solar year.

the northern reaches of Mesoamerica at La Quemada and Alta Vista in Zacatecas state and at Cerro de Huistle in Jalisco. This people, identified by scholars as belonging to the Chalcihuites culture, built a court with colonnades, using both square and round columns, a plaza with pillars and a very large I-shaped ball court. They carved militaristic images of warriors with shields and weapons and they used skull racks as well as – at Cerro de Huistle – an early form of the *chacmool*.

Scholars believe that the sites predated the rise of Tollán and the Chalcihuites culture might therefore have been the precursor of many of the militaristic sacrificial rituals of the Toltecs and their followers at Chichén Itzá and Tenochtitlán.

Below: Twin shrines occupied the summit of the Templo Mayor in Tenochtitlán. This chacmool demanded sacrificial blood outside the shrine of rain god Tláloc.

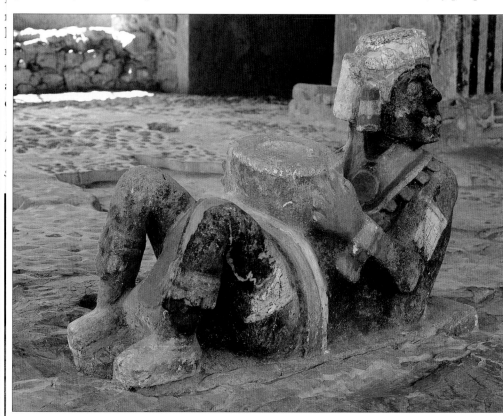

ARE

THE MAGNIFICENCE OF MOCTEZUMA

The mag
Chichén
measuring
including
pitch is I-:
end zone
146m (12
tical side
of which l
its surface

Chiché
part of the
emonial
archaeolog
The city c
courts, th
centre and
great Mes
El Tajín in
were 12 b

As else
had impo
ments. Re
the court
player w
defeated c

Below: The
an exampl
sloping side

Moctezuma's palace in Tenochtitlán was a statement in stone of the *tlatoani's* divine magnificence. Surrounded by extensive gardens containing ponds, court-yards, an aviary and a zoo, the palace was a residence fit for a ruler so magnificent that none of his subjects were permitted to look him in the eye.

ROYAL CITY WITHIN A CITY

Spanish accounts report that Mocte-zuma's palace had more than 300 rooms, which were arranged around internal courtyards. Legal documents concerning landholdings suggest that the emperor's city complex covered 4 hectares (10 acres). An administrative building as well as a royal home, the palace contained military council rooms, a throne room and reception areas for greeting ambas-sadors and political visitors, legal apart-ments used by judges as courtrooms, two armouries and large areas for storing

Below: A reconstruction of Moctezuma's two-storey palace in Tenochtitlán reveals extensive courtyards and gardens within.

tribute from around the empire. Accord-ing to an account by the conquistador Bernal Díaz del Castillo, the palace con-tained extensive areas for storing cacao, feathers, gold, jewels, cotton and foods that had been received as tribute pay-ments. There were also rooms for accountants managing the wealth gener-ated by tribute and taxation.

The vast building contained libraries, music rooms and areas for craftsmen retained to work for the emperor. There were also permanent quarters for the rulers of Texcoco and Tlacopán, the Aztecs' allies in the Triple Alliance, together with guest rooms for visiting notables from states within the empire. The importance of the lakeside town of Chiconauhtla, derived largely from its control over the straits connecting the lakes of Zumpango and Xaltocán with Lake Texcoco, was reflected in the fact that the ruler had the right to keep an apartment in the imperial palace

The Tenochtitlán palace complex was arranged over two floors, with the *tla-toani's* quarters on the upper floor and

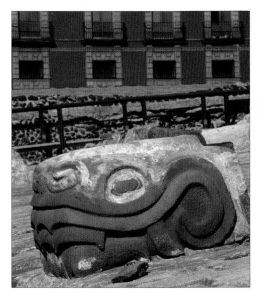

Above: A serpent-head Tenochtitlán foundation stone was uncovered by archaeologists in Mexico City.

state or administrative rooms and ser-vants' living space on the gloomier ground level. An image from the *Codex Mendoza* (c.1541) represents the two-storey build-ing with a courtyard and steps leading to an upper-floor reception room in which the dazzling Moctezuma himself sits in state. On either side of his quarters stand apartments for leading allied rulers. Below on the ground floor lie two meeting rooms, in one of which four judges dis-cuss an important case, while the other is kept for councils of war.

PALACE COURTROOMS

Friar Bernardino de Sahagún's descrip-tion of the palace in Tenochtitlán indicated that legal administration worked on three levels for nobles, military and commoners. In one room of the palace court, legal experts heard noble disputes and complaints of wrongdoing. Their sanctions included banning an offender from the palace complex, banishing a person from the city or ordering his execution by stoning, hanging or beating; chopping off the hair was a lesser pun-ishment, but greatly feared because it would make a leading member of the *pip-iltin* nobility look like a shaven-headed *macehual* or commoner.

In a palace room named the *tecpilcalli*, leading members of the military dispensed their own justice. In the *teccalco* chamber, commoners could bring disputes and complaints to judgement. The *tlatoani* himself heard difficult cases and took advice from the three most senior judges or *tecuhtlatoque* before passing judgement. Judges faced the strictest sanctions – including execution – if they were found to be corrupt.

ANCIENT AMENITIES
There were more than 100 bathrooms in the *tlatoani's* palace. Several times a day the ruler washed and changed his clothes: he discarded his garments after wearing them once. He lived in great splendour on the palace's second floor, with his two wives and 150 concubines, together with legions of guards and attendants. His servants were housed in their own luxurious apartments.

A large part of the palace was given over to kitchens and food stores. At every meal some 300 guests were served from an extensive menu designed to stimulat-

Below: This stone, once part of Moctezuma's elegant Tenochtitlán palace, shows evidence of having been worked by an Aztec mason.

ing the most jaded palate. Such was the *tlatoani's* splendour that dinner guests were forbidden to watch him engage in activities such as eating: he consumed his food in isolation behind a golden screen. Delicacies to tempt the royal diners included frogs served with green chilli peppers, sage-doused locusts and a helping of prickly pear served with fish eggs from the great lake of Texcoco.

In the patios of the royal palace complex, acrobats and musicians practised. The gardens contained ten pools stocked with waterfowls that feasted on fish. Hernán Cortés wrote to King Carlos V of Spain that these birds were so numerous they required 110kg (250lb) of fish each day. In the zoo, royal jaguars, coyotes and

Above: The Codex Mendoza (c.1541) shows Moctezuma sitting on the upper floor of his two-storey palace, between apartments for visiting dignitaries. Before the building, one man departs while four litigants present a case to the judges in the lower right-hand chamber. The lower left-hand chamber is identified as the war council room.

serpents were kept in regal luxury. Some were fed on human flesh carried from the temple complex nearby.

Throughout the palace, servants, guards and administrators burned incense and sweet-smelling woods in their braziers to mask the smell of decaying body parts that the breeze sometimes carried across from the temple quarters.

CHAPTER EIGHT

BUILDING THE CITIES

The builders of great Mesoamerican centres looked for inspiration in the cities and sacred buildings of the past. They paid homage to the achievements of their ancestors by reproducing their styles: Teotihuacáno *talud-tablero* construction spread across Mesoamerica – being used, for instance, in Tikal, Kaminaljuyú, Xochicalco, El Tajín and Chichén Itzá. Great cities of the past were also places of pilgrimage or sacred occupation.

Cities had a unifying function, linking cultures and peoples across centuries, but also connecting people within a region. A city was the focus of its area, providing employment in outlying artisanal areas or an outlet for the excess agricultural produce of the region's farmers. For instance, Tikal provided a means of living for a vast outlying population of some 60,000; Teotihuacán similarly supported a large outer area of rural settlements, some growing food, others working local flint or obsidian; Tenochtitlán was the focus of an extensive area of *chinampa* farmlands.

A city also created connections between areas across great distances: from before the start of the Classic Period, Mesoamerican trade was driven by the needs of wealthy city populations and religious elites for rare or exotic products. Long-distance trade driven by the vast population of Teotihuacán, for instance, forged links across many thousands of kilometres between the Mexican highlands and settlements such as Tikal or Kaminaljuyú.

Left: The North Platform bounds the northern edge of Monte Albán's Plaza, at the heart of Mesoamerica's first true city.

SACRED TOWNS:
SAN LORENZO AND LA VENTA

Settlers first occupied the plateau that became the Olmec centre of San Lorenzo, near the Gulf Coast of Mexico, *c*.1500BC. Their descendants began public building works about 250 years later. A group had grown wealthy and powerful controlling the farming of fertile lands alongside the local Coatzacoalcos and Chiquito rivers and perhaps by managing trade in obsidian, greenstone and basalt from resource-rich uplands nearby. The leader of this group was able to command and reward the labour needed to build a sacred ceremonial centre.

Below: Stela 2 at La Venta shows an Olmec monarch dressed as a player with the bat used in some versions of the game, after c.1000BC.

SACRED CENTRE
Beginning *c*.1250BC, hundreds of workers built up and levelled the plateau. On its top, 50m (160ft) above the surrounding countryside, they laid out a series of pyramids and rectangular courts on a north to south alignment, oriented precisely 8 degrees west of true north – probably to line up with the rising of a star or planet at a ritually significant time such as an equinox. They used clay and earth to make these buildings, but imported basalt from the Tuxtla mountains 70km (10 miles) away to line a remarkable series of drains that were connected to fountains and artificial ponds. These were made from skilfully shaped interconnecting pieces of basalt.

Above: On Altar 5 at La Venta, a king or shaman-priest wearing a jaguar headdress holds a 'were jaguar' baby – an infant with snarling jaguar features.

SACRED FIGUREHEAD
The king may have been worshipped. Eight colossal basalt carved heads erected at San Lorenzo were probably portraits of the settlement's rulers. Some of the heads were more than 3m (10ft) tall and weighed 20 tons. The king's power derived not just from his wealth, but also because he was a sacred figurehead, guarantor of his people's safety and of the

---

RELIGIOUS PIONEERS IN TWIN OLMEC SETTLEMENTS
Olmec remains at San Lorenzo and La Venta suggest that the inhabitants of these temple towns were pioneers in many facets of Mesoamerican religious life. The Olmec worshipped a feathered serpent deity together with a rain god and revered jaguars and eagles as well as crocodiles and sharks. They also practised the rites of autosacrifice, in which a worshipper expelled his or her own blood: stingray spines and other items – perhaps including shark's teeth – were used to induce blood flow. Generations of Mesoamericans would follow the Olmec lead in these matters.

continued fertility of their maize fields. The buildings and monuments of San Lorenzo were erected before 900BC. While the site appears to have been a busy trading settlement after that date, its people did not feel the need to raise further pyramid-mounds or to carve new stone thrones or heads. Some time during the years 900–700BC, axe-wielding men smashed the Olmec heads and thrones of San Lorenzo and buried the remnants in ditches. The violence done to the statues suggests that this was an act of vandalism by invaders, but the careful collection and hiding of the remnants in ditches might indicate that it was a piece of elegiac destruction by Olmec who wanted to set their own age apart from the past.

Pottery remnants from the years after 700BC suggest that at this time San Lorenzo was occupied by people originating in Maya regions of Chiapas and Guatemala. In the years 600–400BC, the inhabitants of the settlement probably built a ball court. Archaeologists have discovered two elongated mounds running in parallel that they believe are the side walls or spectators' stands of a ball court.

AMID THE MARSHES: LA VENTA

From c.1150BC onwards, Olmec builders constructed another centre at La Venta, about 60km (35 miles) north-east of San Lorenzo and just 12km (7 miles) inland from the Gulf coast. They chose a salt mound amid freshwater marshland, in an area where villagers had already been living for more than a millennium, supporting themselves by fishing, hunting, gathering and growing maize in the fertile soil.

La Venta's builders raised a ceremonial centre of mounds and plazas, aligned like those at San Lorenzo precisely 8 degrees to the west of true north. The tallest of these, called Complex C by archaeologists, is an earthen mound 32m (105ft) high. Some scholars have suggested that it was intended as a recreation of a sacred volcano. Others have likened its shape to that of the pyramid in the Group E complex at the later Maya city of Uaxactún, which may have been structured in four quadrants to celebrate the cardinal points and which was aligned precisely to the sun's rising on sacred equinoctial dates. In front of the mound, running north-west, lay an elongated plaza. Beyond the plaza lay a further sacred arena (named

Left: Olmec religious life appears to have centred on worship of the ruler and his ancestors. This colossal basalt head, from La Venta, may represent a departed king.

Above: The four sides of La Venta Altar 5 are carved with shaman-kings holding 'were jaguar' babies. The 'were jaguar' may have been venerated as an image of the rain god.

Complex A by archaeologists) containing a court enclosed on two sides by basalt columns, ten further mounds, several platforms and a buried serpentine mosaic pavement measuring 4.5 by 6m (15 by 20ft) and representing the face of a jaguar, beneath which many sacred offerings were laid. Above the pavement, at ground level, lay a sarcophagus of sandstone carved to represent the earth monster in the form of a crocodile floating on water.

Both La Venta and San Lorenzo were relatively small in size. With around 1,000 people resident in each at their peak, the settlements are perhaps better called towns than cities. For many years archaeologists concentrated on the ceremonial role of La Venta and San Lorenzo, but recent work has established that the sites were residential as well as religious centres. At La Venta, living quarters lay to the north-east of the main ceremonial complex. At San Lorenzo the network of drains may have been used functionally by the town's inhabitants, or may have played a role in religious ceremonies celebrating the life-giving power of the waters that fed the maize plants.

CITY OF THE ZAPOTECS:
MONTE ALBÁN

An elite group among the Zapotec inhabitants of the highland Valley of Oaxaca founded the settlement of Monte Albán *c*.500BC. It was located in a dominant position on a flattened mountain ridge between two peaks, with good views down all three arms of the valley. In its early years, the settlement consisted of three residential districts and contained up to 7,200 people. The ridge had no agricultural land, and Monte Albán's residents lived on the produce of the three arms of Oaxaca valley: Tlacolula to the east, Etla to the north and Zaachila

to the south. Produce was distributed at a market on the flattened ridge. The settlement grew rapidly. Home to 15,000 people by *c*.200BC, Monte Albán had become Mesoamerica's first city.

Major building works had begun about a century earlier, *c*.300BC. An army of labourers flattened the uneven mountaintop and laid out a plaza paved in white stucco.

The Temple of the Danzantes, adorned with carvings of defeated war captives, arose in the south-west corner of the plaza. The city's elite commissioned stone tombs for their burials and builders produced increasingly elaborate masonry graves, some of which were distinguished by corbelled roofs.

Above: Looking north across the expansive Main Plaza at Monte Albán, Building H looms in the foreground.

A MATURE CITY

Monte Albán was a thriving city for several centuries. In the period AD500–750, its population rose as high as 24,000. The city spread over two adjacent hilltops, covering 6.5km (4 miles), and contained 14 residential areas. Each had its own plaza, while the city's elite rulers and administrators lived in 14 'palaces' arranged around the city's main commercial plaza. In these years, labourers erected a great pyramid 15m (50ft) in height and more than 100m (325ft) in length at the south end of the main plaza. Carved stelae at the four corners appear to commemorate a state visit by emissaries from Teotihuacán, perhaps on the occasion of the building's ceremonial dedication. At the northern end of the plaza, builders constructed a hall with fine colonnades that gave on to a low-level patio backed by tall pyramids.

The city specialized in crafts, making elite produce from obsidian and seashells: The workshops lay to the north-east of the main plaza in an area of noble dwellings. The elite of Monte Albán appear to have valued seclusion and privacy. Noble dwellings were secluded, with central patio areas sometimes accessed by long corridors and through a number of intervening rooms. The main plaza was largely cut off from other parts of the city.

Below: A plan of Monte Albán's Main Plaza. The plaza was laid out and paved in white stucco by Zapotec labourers c.300BC.

CAPITAL OF THE BALL GAME:
EL TAJÍN

The settlement of El Tajín in the Gulf Coast region of northern Veracruz was established in the early Classic Period, when it had trading links with the great metropolis of Teotihuacán. The celebrated remains, which include the Pyramid of the Niches and no fewer than 12 ball courts, date from much later – the 9th–11th centuries AD. These remnants are a small part of the city that once stood here: ruins untouched by archaeologists and so still covered in foliage stretch for 5km (3 miles) into the low hills of the surrounding tropical rainforest.

PYRAMID OF THE NICHES
Builders erected the ceremonial centre that contains the Pyramid of the Niches in the flat southern part of city. The six-tier pyramid supports a temple on its flat top, making seven levels in all, with progressively fewer niches in each level. The bottom tier contains 88 niches, the second has 76, then the levels contain 64, 52, 40 and 28 while the temple has 17 – making a total of 365, one for each day of the solar year. Close by, the builders set out two ball courts. One is decorated with bas-relief carving depicting the sacrificial slaughter of a ball player.

Below: Building 3 stands directly west of the Pyramid of the Niches in central El Tajín. It makes use of niches and Teotihuacáno talud-tablero *architectural elements.*

Above: The buildings of El Tajín were at one time covered with polychrome stucco. The niches of the Pyramid of the Niches were painted red with turquoise borders.

Labourers cut terraces into the small hills to the north of the ceremonial centre and laid out an extensive residential area. They raised elite homes or palaces with colonnades, rooms with corbelled vaults and fine roof combs. They built walls to separate the residential district – known as Tajín Chico – from the ceremonial area to the south and from the king's palace complex to the west.

HOME FIT FOR A KING
Skilled stonemasons cut splendid ornate reliefs in the Building of the Columns, one of the main structures in the royal complex, depicting images of military conquest and sacrificial ritual. The ruler shown most frequently in this area is King 13-Rabbit. Images represent toads as well as sacred serpents and royal jaguars. Glyphs indicate that the people of El Tajín followed the 260-day cycle as well as the calendar of 365 days celebrated in the niches of the main pyramid. The wet season in this part of Mexico hits hard: to prevent flooding and conserve water, builders dug elaborate drains, underground waterways and tanks for storage. The city's 12 ball courts have led scholars to speculate that it might have been a centre for playing the ball game – perhaps a site used for grand enactments of sacred ritual linked to calendrical observations.

CAPITAL OF THE TOTONACS?
El Tajín might have been an early capital of the Totonacs, a people who rose to greater prominence in the Postclassic Period in Veracruz and the northern part of Puebla. In the 16th century, the Totonacs – who by then had their capital at Cempoala, some 150km (90 miles) south of El Tajín – had the distinction of becoming the first Mesoamerican people to join Hernán Cortés in his military action against Tenochtitlán.

TOWERING MONUMENTS:
TIKAL

In the dense jungle of the Petén region, Tikal began to expand from a village *c.*500–300BC. By 300AD it was a major city, celebrating in stone the achievements of a great dynasty of kings. At its greatest extent in the 8th century AD, the city – with extensive environs covering about 16sq km (6sq miles) – was home to a population of 60,000.

CYCLICAL REBUILDING
The building of Tikal was a massive feat of construction. The main temples, tombs, ceremonial buildings and elite residences covered 2.5sq km (1sq mile). Moreover, most of the city's main buildings were refashioned and reconstructed many times. By Mesoamerican tradition, new structures were erected directly above and encompassing their predecessors. In Tikal, the building of the North Acropolis, a collection of pyramid temple-tombs, began as early as 250BC. Over the centuries the Acropolis floor was re-laid 20 times, so that the final layer was a full 10m (33ft) higher than the first. Scholars believe that the city must have supported a full-time force of stonemasons, sculptors, painters and labourers to carry out this cyclical building and rebuilding.

The centre of the ceremonial complex was the Great Plaza. To its north lay the North Acropolis, burial ground of kings. Many times rebuilt, it consisted in its final form of a large rectangular platform, 100m by 80m (325ft by 260ft), supporting eight royal temple-tombs built *c.*AD250–550. Subsequently, four further temples were built on a second platform along the southern extremity of the North Acropolis, giving via stairways on to the Great Plaza.

TWIN MORTUARY MONUMENTS
Facing one another on the eastern and western sides of the Great Plaza rose Temple I and Temple II. Temple I, which climbs in nine terraces to a height of 50m (164ft) on the eastern side, was built as

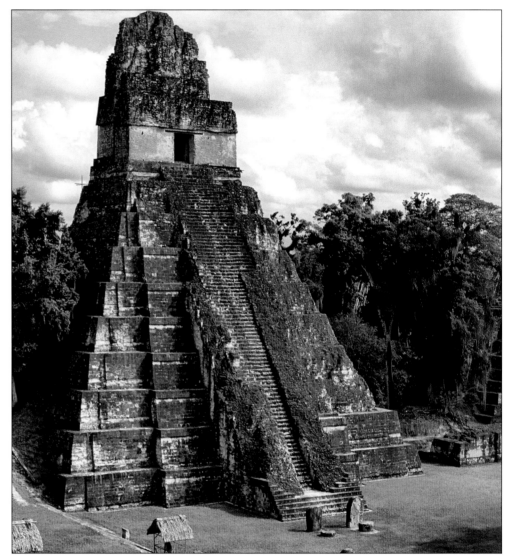

the funerary temple of King Ah Cacau (AD682–734). He was the first member of Tikal's dynasty to be buried outside the North Acropolis. Temple II, rising in three levels to a height of 42m (138ft), supports a sacred building that might have been set up to honour Ah Cacau's queen: the remains of a wooden lintel from this temple bear a portrait of a royal woman.

To the west and east of the Great Plaza lay other plazas. Behind Temple I lay the East Plaza, containing a ball court and a rectangular collection of buildings thought to have been used as a market. From the East Plaza, a *sacbé* known to archaeologists as the Mendez Causeway

Above: The stairs leading to the summit of Temple I rise at an angle of more than 70°.

led south-east past a collection of palaces now called Group G for 0.5 km (0.3 miles) to Temple VI. This temple is also known as the Temple of the Inscriptions because stonemasons carved a record of Tikal's dynastic history on the rear and sides of the roof comb that rose above its summit temple. Labourers built Temple VI during or just after the reign of Ah Cacau's son, Yax Kin (AD734–46). A stela celebrating Yax Kin's accession was erected at the foot of the great pyramid. South of the East Plaza was the Central

Acropolis, a vast palace containing buildings arranged around courtyards. This was probably the official residence of Tikal's ruling dynasty. Farther south beyond one of the city's many reservoirs rose Temple V, Tikal's second tallest structure at 57m (185ft), the temple-tomb of an as yet unidentified ruler. This southernmost region of the ceremonial centre also included another area of royal tombs, the South Acropolis, and the Plaza of the Seven Temples, which in addition to seven temple-shrines gave on to numerous palaces to south and west. It contained a triple ball court, with three pitches, which is unique in Mesoamerica. Beyond this plaza to the west, labourers built the Lost World complex, which contained a platform on its western edge and three platforms on its eastern side aligned with equinoctial sunrises – like the Group E arrangement of pyramids in the Maya city of Uaxactún.

Behind Temple II, a *sacbé* now known as the Tozzer Causeway led westwards to Temple IV, 70m (230ft) high and the tallest building in Tikal. This structure was built for King Yax Kin (AD734–746). Two surviving wooden lintels above the

Below: This view of the North Acropolis is from the heights of Temple I.

doorway to the temple-shrine on the summit of the artificial mountain record the date 9.15.10.0.0. in the Maya Long Count (AD741). A *sacbé* now called the Maudslay Causeway ran north to a collection of twin pyramid groups.

Temple III, which lay to the south of the Tozzer Causeway, was the last pyramid temple erected at Tikal. It was probably the mortuary shrine of King Chitam (AD768–794). A stela erected at its base was carved with the date 9.19.0.0.0. (AD810). Only one later dated monument was raised at Tikal, a stela of 10.2.0.0.0. (AD869) in the Great Plaza. By the end of the 9th century the city had been abandoned to the encroaching vegetation and to groups of squatters.

TWIN PYRAMID GROUPS

At Tikal, several rulers erected twin pyramid groups to mark the close of a *katun* or period of twenty 360-day years (a total of 7,200 days). The groups consisted of

Above: Four sacbeob *(causeways) link groups of sacred buildings in central Tikal.*

two pyramids, each with a flat top and four access stairways, symmetrically arranged on the west and east edges of a plaza, with an enclosure containing an altar and a stela on the plaza's northern edge and a building with nine doorways on its southern edge. These groups have been found only at Tikal, save examples at Yaxha and Ixlu. The first at Tikal was erected in the early years of the 6th century AD in the East Plaza and reused several times. In the late 7th century AD, King Ah Cacau (AD682–734) erected a twin pyramid group to celebrate the end of the first *katun* following his accession. Its altar was marked with the date 9.13.0.0.0. (18 March AD692). From this occasion until AD790, a new group was erected for each *katun*-ending. The largest (known as Twin-Pyramid Group 4E-4) was built in AD771 by King Chitam.

PACAL'S GLORY:
PALENQUE

The city of Palenque at the northern edge of the Chiapas highlands in Mexico, site of the ornate 7th-century tomb of King Pacal that is one of the glories of Mesoamerica, was distinctly different from Tikal and other great Maya cities of the Classic Period.

It contained no forests of carved stelae, no wide ceremonial plazas, no great *sacbé* or causeways, no acropolis of royal tombs. Its buildings were adorned with stucco sculpture and carved reliefs that pioneered naturalistic portraiture of royal figures. It gave pride of place at the centre of the city to the royal palace, home of the living king, rather than – as at Tikal – to temple-tombs housing the remains of divine ancestors.

Palenque appears to have risen to a position of power in the reign of King Pacal (*r.* AD615–83). Most of the surviving parts of the city date from his reign or later and the oldest surviving use of the city's emblem glyph was cut during his time.

PACAL'S PIONEERS
Pacal began a major programme of building in AD647, raising the temple Olvidado ('Unnoticed Shrine'), around half a kilometre to the south of the palace in the city centre. His architect-builders pioneered the use of the thin walls and numerous wide doorways that would become a distinctive feature of Palenque architecture. The temple, standing on an

Above: The lid of Pacal's sarcophagus shows the king falling down the cross-shaped Tree of Life into the underworld.

escarpment and reached by four stretches of stairs linked by platforms, had three doorways giving on to two inner rooms. Inscriptions on the north façade, carved within round cartouches, identified the king as the son of his father, Kan-Bahlum Mo', and of his mother, Lady Zac-Kuk.

THE KING'S PALACE
Pacal proceeded to develop the palace complex. On the large palace platform originally constructed by his predecessors, he built the royal residences identified as Houses E, C, B and A and laid out the expansive East Court. He commissioned sculptors to decorate the palace walls with stucco portrait masks, hieroglyphs, supernatural symbols and sacred scenes. To the south he began work

Left: In the eastern part of the city centre, the temples of the Cross, the Foliated Cross and the Sun celebrated Pacal's dynasty.

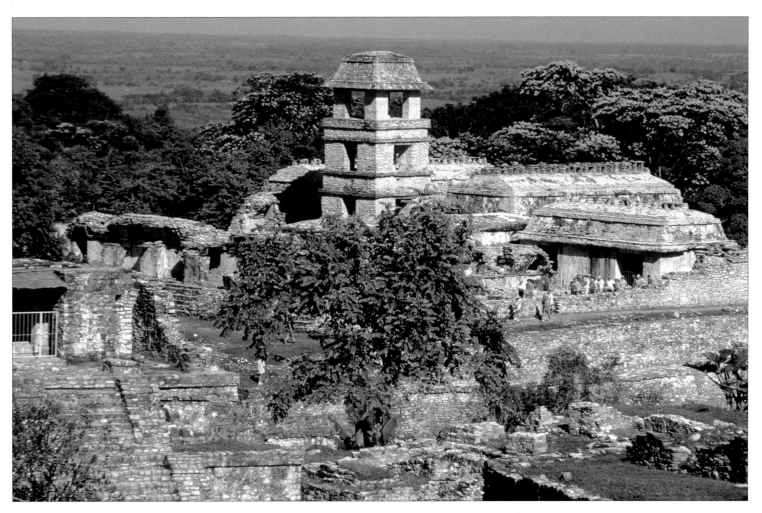

Above: The Palace tower at Palenque commands wide-ranging views of the green Chiapas countryside.

on the great Temple of the Inscriptions, beneath which his tomb was prepared, ready for his eventual death in AD683.

Pacal's son Chan-Bahlum (*r.* AD684–702) completed the Temple of the Inscriptions, which rose to a height of 25m (82ft) and was topped with a temple containing five wide doorways and a roof comb. The portions of the temple facing the court were decorated with painted stucco reliefs that depicted the new king receiving his divine sanction to rule from great Pacal.

POWER OF THE ROYAL LINE

Next, Chan-Bahlum erected three shrines – the Temple of the Cross, the Temple of the Foliated Cross and the Temple of the Sun – facing one another across a plaza in the eastern part of the city centre. They each represented one of the three levels of the Maya universe. The Temple of the Cross, situated in the north, was linked to the heavens; the Temple of the Foliated Cross, in the easterly direction of the rising sun, was associated with the earth; and the Temple of the Sun, in the westerly direction of the setting sun, was identified with the underworld. They contained carvings celebrating Chan-Bahlum's links to his divine father.

A panel in the Temple of the Cross showed Pacal and Chan-Bahlum on either side of the ceiba world tree that the Maya believed connected the three levels of the universe. The carving in the Temple of the Foliated Cross depicted the pair on either side of a giant cob of maize bearing human heads, a reference to the Maya creation myth in which the gods Huracán and Gucumatz made the first humans from maize. The image in the Temple of the Sun presented Chan-Bahlum and his father adopting a martial pose, one to each side of a battle shield adorned with spears and the jaguar god of the underworld.

Archaeologists have not found Chan-Bahlum's tomb, but many believe it may lie beneath the Temple of Cross since this was the northern member of the group and burials were generally laid in the direction of the north.

Chan-Bahlum II's brother, Kan-Xul II, rebuilt the palace complex and may have erected the curious four-storey tower that was probably an astronomical observatory. This structure has no counterpart anywhere else in the Maya realm. Scholar Linda Schele has suggested that the tower was built as a tribute to King Pacal. An observer standing at the top of the tower at the winter solstice would see the sun set directly on to the Temple of the Inscriptions, thus going down into the underworld by way of Pacal's tomb.

With Kan-Xul II's reign the great building work of Palenque came to a close: the king was captured in AD711 by the rival city of Toniná and, after a long captivity, was beheaded there. Before the century was out, Palenque became one of the first Maya cities to cease cutting dates in inscriptions and so enter the historical silence of the celebrated collapse of the 8th and 9th centuries. The last inscribed date at Palenque was AD799.

CITY OF THE JAGUAR KINGS:
YAXCHILÁN

Yaxchilán was built on a hill overlooking a bend in the Usumacinta river in Chiapas, Mexico. The city's origins lie in the 4th century AD, when it may have been founded as a satellite of Tikal, but it was developed primarily by two kings of the 8th century: Lord Shield Jaguar (*r.* AD681–742) and his son Bird Jaguar (*r.* AD752–68). From the date of its investigation by Sir Alfred Maudslay, the British gentleman-scholar hailed as the 'father of Maya archaeology', Yaxchilán has been celebrated for its magnificently carved door lintels, some of which have been on display in the British Museum in London since Maudslay had them shipped to Europe in 1882.

TOMB FOR A QUEEN

The city's main ceremonial area lies on an artificial terrace above the Usumacinta. The large plaza runs parallel to the river. On its south side, Lord Shield Jaguar built a structure known to archaeologists as

Below: A detail shows the stone lintels of Yaxchilán's palaces. The remains of a stone throne lie before the building.

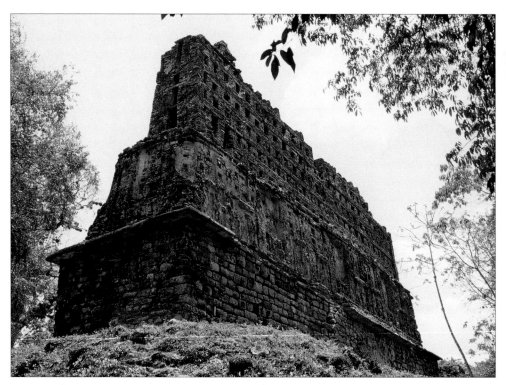

Temple 23, or the Queen's House, that was dedicated to his principal wife, Lady Xoc, in 9.14.14.13.17 (726AD), the 45th year of his 61-year reign. This building contains celebrated door-lintel carvings of Lady Xoc performing rites of ritual bloodletting by running a spiked cord across her tongue; of Lady Xoc having a sacred experience through the Vision Snake of King Yat Balam, founder of the dynasty; and of Shield Jaguar, accompanied by his wife, donning battle garb as he prepared to set out in search of sacrificial captives. Temple 24, erected on the western edge of the Queen's House, recorded her death in AD749 and almost certainly contains her grave.

Earlier, in AD732, the king dedicated Temple 44, also known as the War Memorial as it commemorated a series of noble captives taken by Lord Shield Jaguar. Among other sacred structures erected by Shield Jaguar was Temple 41, at the summit of the hill that rises behind the ceremonial terrace. This structure commemorated celebrations of a sacred solstice in 9.15.9.17.16 (AD741).

Above: Stucco sculptures once decorated the roof of Temple 33. Standing on high ground, the vast temple dominates the city centre.

STRUGGLE TO SUCCEED

Lord Shield Jaguar was succeeded by his son Bird Jaguar. The succession was not without its difficulties. Bird Jaguar was not the king's son by his principal wife, Lady Xoc, but by another royal bride, Lady Evening Star, who is thought by scholars to have come originally from Calakmul. Whether because the succession was contested by a son of Lady Xoc, or because Bird Jaguar's connection to the royal line of Calakmul made him unpopular, there was a gap of ten years between the death of Lord Shield Jaguar in AD742 and the coronation of Bird Jaguar in AD752. Afterwards these difficulties contributed greatly to construction in Yaxchilan's ceremonial quarter: Bird Jaguar erected many buildings and stelae promoting his right to the throne and, once his position was secure, poured his construction efforts into securing the succession of his son Chel Te.

In the course of these projects, Bird Jaguar III rebuilt most of the ceremonial centre and also extended the city to the south-east. Before his time the main plaza was crossed by gullies, but he had the area flattened and smoothed. In a reign of 16 years, he built 12 sacred buildings and raised 33 monuments. Much of the work complemented that of his father. He built a new hilltop structure, Temple 40, alongside Shield Jaguar's Temple 41 and in front raised a carved stela that celebrated both his father and mother and made reference to the solstice celebration of

Below: Bird Jaguar wears an elaborate costume and headdress and holds the manikin *sceptre, symbol of royal authority.*

AD741 in which, as a prince, Bird Jaguar had shared duties with his father. Alongside Temple 23, which his father had built to honour Lady Xoc, Bird Jaguar erected Temple 21, which was adorned with lintels representing Bird Jaguar and his wife enacting the same scenes celebrated in the lintels of the earlier temple. One showed Bird Jaguar watching a wife letting blood from a tongue, another showed a wife encountering the Vision Serpent and a third showed Bird Jaguar in his military glory.

LINTEL RECORDS

Behind Temple 23, Bird Jaguar built another sacred building, known as Temple 33, where the steps were carved with scenes of rituals involving the ball game: one showed Bird Jaguar enacting a sacrifice with noble victims bound in the form of balls from the ball game. On the lintel above the temple doorway, Bird Jaguar rose in his full glory at his accession, dressed in the costume of a Maya king and holding the *manikin* sceptre. Other lintels at the temple depict Bird Jaguar and his son performing a ritual and Bird Jaguar again in the company of a leading noble. Many of the nobles of Bird Jaguar's reign are represented in door-lintel carvings and on stelae: scholars suggest that the king may have needed support in order to consolidate his position and so was forced to share status with these lords by including them in the historical record.

PRIDE OF THE TOLTECS:
TOLLÁN

The celebrated home of the Toltecs was an extensive city encompassing some 13km (8 miles). Its population of up to 60,000 was spread out in outlying areas and lived by farming, mining basalt, making chert tools and working obsidian. The ceremonial area at the centre was precisely laid out 18 degrees east of north. It contained two pyramids, two plazas, a council hall and two ball courts.

The most important structure, facing on to the main plaza from its eastern edge was the one known as Building C. This was once a pyramid temple platform, but Aztec pilgrims dismantled the temple and removed the stone facing. All that remains is the small mountain of rock and earth that formed the core of the pyramid, together with a few pieces of carved stone. Scholars believe that the temple would have been a modest two-room building with an antechamber and a shrine, but do not know which god was honoured there.

Below: Sacred snakes feast on human skeletons on the coatepantli *or serpent wall that runs along Building B's north side.*

IN QUETZALCÓATL'S HONOUR

To the north of the plaza, Toltec builders erected a five-stepped temple pyramid sacred to Quetzalcóatl. On the top of the pyramid the temple roof was supported by columns, some in the shape of warriors 3.5m (11ft) tall. Before the temple, a reclining *chacmool* would have been placed. The warrior figures were broken up and cast into a ditch, perhaps by looters, but have been reassembled and returned to their place of duty on the top of the pyramid.

Stonemasons cut panels to face the tiers of the pyramid. They represented a human head emerging from a monster's jaws, an image tentatively identified as Quetzalcóatl Tlahuizcalpantecuhtli, the god in his form as Venus the Morning Star. They also showed eagles, jaguars and coyotes consuming human hearts. Traces of paint sometimes show that these would have been painted bright colours.

THE BURNT PALACE

To the east of the temple lay a secular building that archaeologists call the Palace of Quetzalcóatl or Edificio 1, while to the west was a vast building measuring 59m

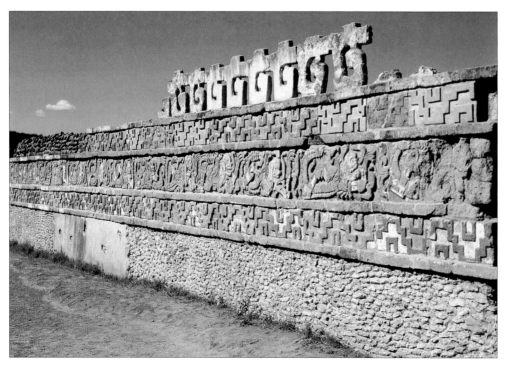

Above: Atlantean figures on the Temple of Quetzalcóatl. Their eyes and mouths were probably inlaid with obsidian or shell.

by 91m (200ft by 300ft) and called the Palacio Quemado – or 'Burnt Palace', because it was largely consumed by flames. Its builders set it out in three halls with colonnades that face south on to a long gallery. The Burnt Palace was probably an administrative building used for meetings, receptions and storing trade and tribute items. Gamblers would have gathered there to play *patolli*: three boards for the game are marked on the floor.

In the west of the central area lay a ball court and the space between the main plaza and the court was probably the marketplace. In the centre of the main plaza stood a square shrine around 1.7m (5ft 6in) tall, built in the *talud-tablero* style of Teotihuacán and with one staircase on each of its four sides.

TWIN STYLES:
CHICHÉN ITZÁ

The main buildings of Chichén Itzá were laid out in two styles in different areas of the city. Three structures, mainly in the Puuc architectural style, later called the Nunnery, the Annex and the Iglesia occupied the southernmost part of central Chichén Itzá. The Akabdzib, a building in similar style to the east of this group, has been dated to *c.*AD869. To the west lay the Casa Colorado or 'Red House', with a frieze commemorating noble bloodletting ceremonies in AD869 and AD870.

North-east of the Nunnery group, lay the curious circular building later called the Caracol (from the Spanish for snail) because the spiral staircase within it was held to resemble a snail's shell. A stela found on the building's upper platform dated it to AD906. It may have been a circular temple or an observatory.

THE NORTHERN COMPLEX
A *sacbé* ran northwards from the Caracol to the northern group of buildings, comprising the Temple of Kukulcán, the Temple of the Warriors, a ball court and the Group of the Thousand Columns. The complex was arranged precisely 18 degrees east of true north.

Above: Puuc-style buildings were in the south, Toltec-style structures in the north.

HOLY WATERS
The city made use of two major *cenotes* or natural wells formed when the limestone rock in the area collapsed to reveal water gathered beneath. One, the Xtoloc *cenote*, lay in the centre of the city, to the east of the causeway linking the Caracol to the northern platform. The second, the *Cenote* of Sacrifice, was the site of human sacrifice and other ritual offerings and lay to the north of the northern platform.

Left: Puuc-style carving on the facade of the Nunnery represent the the earth monster and the long-nosed rain god Chac.

HILL FORTS:
CACAXTLA, XOCHICALCO AND TEOTENANGO

In the central highlands around the Basin of Mexico, three fortified hilltop settlements flourished from the 7th and 8th centuries AD onward, at the time that Teotihuacán and Monte Albán were in decline. Historians believe that as the powers of Teotihuacán and Monte Albán waned, the highland cities began to reassert their influence. The cities of Cacaxtla, overlooking the Tlaxcala valley, Xochicalco in western Morelos and Teotenango in the Toluca valley exhibited a common style in the use of glyphs and counting systems. The first two cities largely faded from prominence after AD900, but Teotenango was an important independent centre until its conquest by the Aztec *tlatoani* Axayácatl in 1476.

CACAXTLA
Celebrated for its mural paintings, Cacaxtla rose to prominence after *c.*AD650 in a well-appointed hilltop location that had been occupied since the Preclassic Period. The hill on which Cacaxtla stood

would have been an obvious choice for settlement, for it enjoyed a plentiful water supply from its own springs and was an easily defended position commanding views of the Tlaxcala valley and beyond.

Archaeologists have discovered that there were at least five stages of construction at Cacaxtla. Its builders laid out the ceremonial site on the hilltop on a rough north–south axis. They erected a palace, temple-shrines, altars and several corridor-like structures. The corridors were part of a distinctive construction thought to be associated with the system of defences: a series of long, low buildings arranged around patios over several levels and joined by staircases, which would have been easily defended in times of conflict.

Cacaxtla's patios and doorways were the sites of human offerings, mainly of babies and children: 208 skeletons have been found, including those of 199 infants. These scores of young lives were probably offered as dedication sacrifices when the buildings were completed. In the sacrifices the bones were scattered randomly, together with obsidian points and scrapers, shells, figurines of animals,

Above: On Xochicalco's Temple of the Feathered Serpent, Quetzalcóatl is represented with consuming jaws.

bone needles and jewellery such as ear spools and nose plugs. From the main patio of the ceremonial area, steps led up to an elongated chamber with seven entrances painted with vividly coloured murals depicting battle scenes. The conflict might portray a ritualized bloodletting. Warriors wearing Teotihuacán-style outfits defeat others identified as Maya by their deliberately deformed heads. Some of the Maya are naked and painted turquoise blue, the traditional colour of sacrifice.

A stairway from the chamber led to a structure now called Building A by archaeologists, which was dominated by four large painted figures on either side of the doorway. One figure, believed to represent the moon, is depicted as a jaguar-man releasing drops of life-giving water from a sceptre on to the prone body of a jaguar-serpent. Another figure, in similar costume, pours water from a pot marked with symbols of the rain god Tláloc.

In the south-west of the ceremonial centre builders erected what appears to be a temple to Venus the Morning Star (Tlahuizcalpantecuhtli). On either side of a doorway artists painted two large figures, each wearing a five-pointed half-star that was a well known symbol of Venus.

Below: The South Plaza at Teotenango appears to have been laid out as a homage to the Ciudadela or Citadel in Teotihuacán.

XOCHICALCO

At Xochicalco, builders cut deep ditches, walls and ramps to fortify much of the lower part of the hill and laid out the residential and ceremonial areas of the settlement on terraces cut into the upper slopes. They built causeways to connect areas of the site and to link the city to

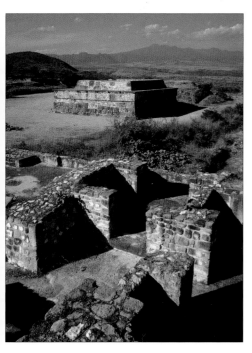

Above: This blue-skinned toad appears in Cacaxtla's Red Temple. The plant behind him bears 'fruit' of human heads.

nearby settlements. One connected the ceremonial and residential hilltop to the ball court, which was laid out on the lower hill with rings on the side walls.

In the main ceremonial area, artisans carved the Pyramid of the Feathered Serpent with images of high-ranking warriors and lists of places that paid tribute to the city's military hierarchy, together with Feathered Serpent reliefs and glyphs relating to fire ceremonies and to the ritual calendar. About 30m (100ft) south of the pyramid, workers built a sacred structure now called the Temple of the Stelae, because it contained three expertly carved stone posts, each bearing a human face and a set of glyphs. Scholars still debate the meaning of these stelae. Some suggest that they represent sky and fertility deities and were used in

Left: The Temple of the Feathered Serpent stands in the centre of the main square in Xochicalco, laid out on a terraced acropolis.

agricultural rites. Others claim that they were, like the carving on the pyramid, a celebration of Xochicalco's military might. The stelae were deliberately damaged and broken, then buried in pieces, but scholars have gathered the fragments and put them back together.

TEOTENANGO

At Teotenango the land falls away sharply from the hilltop on three sides, while on its northern edge labourers erected a vast defensive wall. On the hilltop, from about AD750 onwards, settlers laid out a large ritual and civic area with a number of plazas, altars, temple platforms, a ball court, residential areas, streets and markets. The builders were clearly influenced by Teotihuacán and paid tribute in their own construction to the architecture and sculptural achievements of that great city. In particular, the South Plaza at Teotenango, enclosed by low buildings with stairways, appears to be a reproduction of the great Citadel at Teotihuacán. Teotenango's highest building was the Temple of the Serpent, adorned with serpent carvings.

TARASCAN STRONGHOLD:
TZINTZUNTZAN

The Tarascans laid out their capital, Tzintzuntzan, beneath wooded highlands on the shores of Lake Pátzcuaro in Michoacán, western Mexico, at an altitude of 2,130m (7,000ft). An army of labourers, probably prisoners or workers provided as tribute by peoples humbled in the course of the Tarascans' empire-building wars, created a vast east-facing terrace measuring 440m by 260m (1,440ft by 850ft). Here they built, in line, five temples on terraced circular platforms. The temples have been destroyed but the platforms, called *yácatas*, remain. They were faced with great slabs of stone.

Nearby, the Tarascans' labour force raised a building now known as El Palacio, with many rooms arranged around a patio together with a roofed, narrow gallery defined by rectangular pillars. This might have been a royal palace or a residential area for elite priests, conveniently situated close to the temples supported by the *yácatas*.

A KING'S TEMPLE BURIAL?

The *yácata* temple mounds might also have been mortuary monuments. Archaeologists found graves they believe to be sacrificial burials of servants in the mound they call Yácata V. One grave, in the south-east corner, contained five women, buried with copper ornaments,

Below: The yácatas *were faced with stone veneer, which does not survive here. Some 40,000 people once lived in Tzintzuntzan.*

Above: Circular platforms or yacátas *survive at Tzintzuntzan without the temples that once stood on top of them.*

bells and ritual vessels. Another, in the north, contained nine women buried with arms linked together and accompanied by rich deposits including obsidian lip plugs, turquoise ear plugs, silver tweezers and gold earrings, along with copper bells and axes. The burials might have been made to accompany one of the Tarascan kings on his voyage into the afterlife. The royal grave probably lies nearby, but has not yet been found.

HOME OF THE HUMMINGBIRDS

The Tarascans were skilled producers of gold and silver jewellery and of copper axe heads. They and their predecessors in western Mexico were the pioneers of metalworking techniques in Mesoamerica, using knowledge and skills passed along trade routes into western Mexico from Colombia and Peru. They were the only Mesoamericans to use metal weapons.

The Tarascans were also known for their high level of skill in weaving, in particular for making mosaics of feathers using the plumes of local hummingbirds. Their capital's name, Tzintzuntzan, meant 'home of the hummingbirds'.

TARASCANS DEFEATED

Tarascan skill in making weapons, together with great martial spirit, kept all-comers at bay. Even the imperial Aztec army in the reign of Axayácatl (1469–81) did not succeed in defeating the people of Tzintzuntzan in 1479. However, in 1522 the Spanish adventurer Captain Olíd, who had served under Cortés in the siege of Tenochtitlán, took the Tarascan capital without a struggle.

When Cortés had been marching on Tenochtitlán in 1519 he had sent emissaries to Tzintzuntzan asking for military help. Rather than send a reply, the king ordered his priests to sacrifice the Spaniards to the gods. However, the Europeans had unwittingly brought a hidden weapon, for a smallpox epidemic swept through the ranks of the Tarascans and carried off the king. When the Spanish returned three years later, the new king did not dare to fight the soldiers who had brought down the Aztecs.

CITY OF PRIESTS:
MITLA

The elegant palaces of Mitla, which lie at an altitude of 1,480m (4,855ft) on the eastern edge of the Tlacolula valley in Oaxaca, were built on an ancient settlement inhabited by Zapotecs from as early as 1200BC. Mitla rose to prominence in the Postclassic Period following the decline of nearby Monte Albán. From *c*.AD900 the Mixtecs left their mark on the site. Archaeologists have found numerous Zapotec tombs at the site, which they believe was a sacred burial place. Its Zapotec name was Lyobaa ('Site of Burials'), while the name of Mitla was Nahuatl for 'Realm of the Dead'.

A CITY LAID OUT
The city was laid out in five groups of thin, elongated structures arranged around rectangular courtyards. Beneath the South Group, which was on the southern bank of the Rio Grande de Mitla, archaeologists found a collection of cruciform tombs with elite burials in them. The

Below: The Hall of the Columns still bears traces of its original colour. It takes its name from the stone pillars standing within it.

other buildings were arranged on the rocky hillside opposite. To the west lay the Arroyo Group and the Adobe Group, while the Group of the Columns sat in the east and the Churches Group occupied the north-east of the settlement. Gravediggers laid out more tombs beneath the Group of the Columns.

INFLUENTIAL MOSAICS
At Mitla, Zapotec craftsmen arranged cut stones in a mosaic to form a decorative fretwork and other geometric patterns on façades and door frames. Architectural historians believe these designs might have been influenced by the development of geometric decoration patterns in the Puuc style of north–central Yucatán.

The Zapotec builders used beams to support the roofs, which were gently sloping, so that rainwater would drain off into the courtyards. They made the walls of mud and stone and covered them with plaster or trachyte.

The Group of the Columns was divided into north and south courtyards. From the North Court there was access through a hall named for its six huge

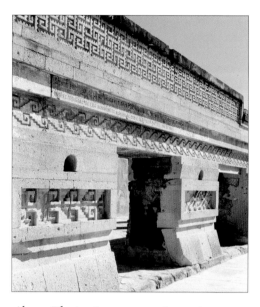

Above: The intricate geometric carving on the outer walls of the Hall of the Columns is remarkably well preserved.

columns to an enclosed courtyard surrounded by four rooms. Historians believe this was the residence of Mitla's priestly elite. The courtyard decorations represent Quetzalcóatl in the form of a stylized celestial serpent. Some of Mitla's rooms were decorated by Mixtec painters.

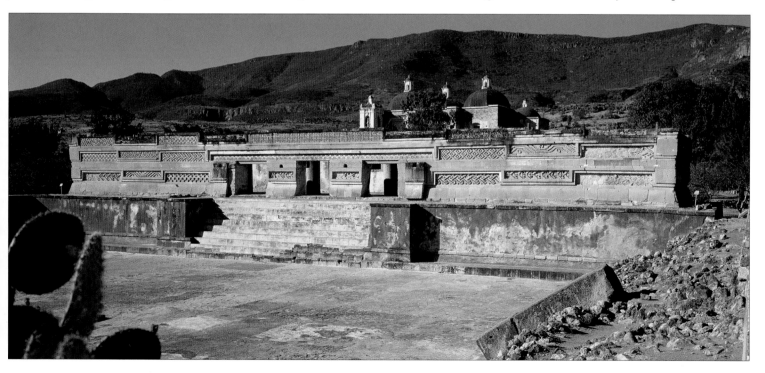

CENTRE OF THE WORLD:
TENOCHTITLÁN

Like the Teotihuacános before them, the Aztecs laid out their capital in four quarters – according to legend, on the command of the tribal lord Huitzilopochtli himself. At the centre stood the vast ceremonial precinct containing the Templo Mayor. Nearby was the great imperial palace and the vast market square of Tlatelolco. Causeways 3.5m (12ft) in width left the island city to north, west and south, connecting the mainland. On the island the causeways became great thoroughfares that terminated in the sacred complex at the city's heart. Fresh water was carried into the city by aqueduct from Coyoacan.

Each of the *capultin* or tribal groups had its own land, with sacred precincts and temple. There were 12–15 *capultin* in each of the four quarters. Major rites and important celebrations were held in the main ceremonial precincts. People moved about on foot or by canoe along the canals that crisscrossed the city.

THE TEMPLE GROUNDS

The sacred quarters of Tenochtitlán were enclosed by a wall in a large square area about 365m (1,200ft) on each side. The wall was known as the *coatepantli* ('Serpent Wall'), because its outside was carved with snake images. At the eastern end the Templo Mayor rose to a height of 45m (150ft), supporting twin temples. On the northern part of the temple platform stood a shrine to Tláloc, with a *chacmool* before it, while on the southern part was the holy place of Huitzilopochtli, before which stood a blood-drenched sacrificial stone.

Climbing towards these temples from ground level, a priest first took a staircase decorated with painted stucco designs honouring the Feathered Serpent Quetzalcóatl and with frogs, which were symbols of Tláloc. The steps led him to a lower platform, on which a vast stone carving of moon goddess Coyolxauhqui was set in the floor before the steps to the Huitzilopochtli shrine. From this place steps rose steeply to the temple above. When a victim's body was cast down from the shrine of Huitzilopochtli, it would fall on the features of the god's mother, Coyolxauhqui. The Templo Mayor was flanked by other sacred structures. To the north were the military

Left: Scholars now believe the temple north of the Templo Mayor to have been the warriors' quarters, the House of Eagles.

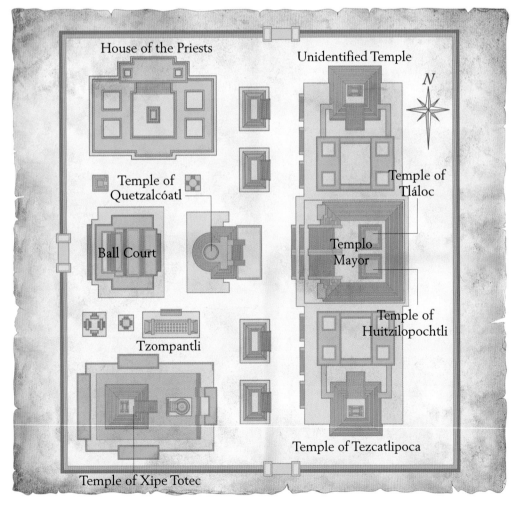

House of the Priests

Unidentified Temple

N

Temple of Quetzalcóatl

Temple of Tláloc

Ball Court

Templo Mayor

Temple of Huitzilopochtli

Tzompantli

Temple of Tezcatlipoca

Temple of Xipe Totec

Above: The vast Templo Mayor, 45m (150ft) tall, dwarfed the rounded temple of Quetzalcóatl-Éhecatl that stood before it.

quarters of elite warriors, called the House of Eagles, while to the south rose a temple to Tezcatlipoca. West of the Templo Mayor stood a circular temple holy to Quetzalcóatl in his guise as wind god Éhecatl and beyond that, at the western limit of the ritual enclosure, was a ball court.

THE TEMPLO MAYOR OVER TIME

The first temple was built *c*.1325, the year of the city's establishment. According to the foundation legend, the México/Aztecs built a rudimentary platform and temple from wattle and daub to honour Huitzilopochtli in the very spot at which they saw an eagle consuming a snake on a cactus, in fulfilment of a divine prophecy. Archaeologists have not been able to uncover evidence of this lowest-level structure. They do know that by *c*.1390, a temple building about 15m (50ft) tall stood on the site. It already supported twin temples to Huitzilopochtli and Tláloc, approached by twin staircases.

Around 1431, three years after the foundation of the Triple Alliance of Tenochtitlán, Texcoco and Tlacopan, the Aztecs built a much larger temple on the same site, entirely enclosing the previously existing structure.

They made further improvements in 1454, under the rule of Moctezuma I (1440–69), adding decorative elements and making many offerings. In particular, builders added a new staircase to the western face of the pyramid and skilled

craftsmen laid a greenstone sculpture of Coyolxauhqui at its foot. This was the forerunner of the celebrated Coyolxauhqui stone, which artisans carved in 1469 under the rule of Axayácatl (1469–81).

Later rulers Tizoc, Ahuítzotl and Moctezuma II demonstrated their devotion by making improvements and additions to the temple in 1482, 1486 and 1502 respectively.

A SACRED SPOT

The México/Aztecs built up their capital in a sanctified setting on twin islands in Lake Texcoco. Setting the city on an island had great religious significance, for it made Tenochtitlán a recreation of the México/Aztecs' legendary northern place of origin, Aztlán, which they believed was

Left: The Codex Durán *represents the twin shrines, to Tláloc and Huitzilopochtli, that occupied the top of the Templo Mayor.*

Right: Sacred precinct in the heart of the city. Hernán Cortés drew this map of Tenochtitlán to send to Charles V.

land surrounded by water. It also meant that the city was a microcosm of the earth itself, a tribute to the gods' creation, for in Aztec cosmology, the earth was surrounded, like a great island, on all sides by water.

WATERWORKS

Tenochtitlán's development was due in no small part to their success in reclaiming the marshy shallows of western Lake Texcoco for *chinampa* fields, and later taking control of the established fields in the southern lakes of Chalco and Xochimilco. In the reign of Moctezuma I (1440–69), labourers built a vast 15km (10-mile) dyke to prevent the salt waters of the northern and eastern part of Lake Texcoco from polluting the freshwater areas that they were farming.

CHAPTER NINE

POTTERS AND WEAVERS

As royal wife Lady Xoc knelt before her kingly husband Shield Jaguar, drawing a spiky rope across her tongue to make a sacred offering of her blood, she wore an exquisitely decorated *huipil* cotton garment. The carver of this celebrated 8th-century scene on a limestone door lintel from Temple 23 in Shield Jaguar's city of Yaxchilán paid great attention to detail – and gave a tantalizing glimpse of the highly developed art of Maya weaving.

Of the work of Mesoamerican potters, weavers, basket-makers, mat-makers and feather-workers covered here, only pots survive in large numbers. This is partly because woven textiles and basket-work naturally decay while ceramic products survive unless smashed, but also because many pots were saved from everyday breakage by being put to sacred use as temple or tomb offerings. Yet although most Maya and many Aztec creations in cloth and basketwork have not survived, we know that they were intricately made and decorated. We have evidence of carved and painted images – both of people wearing woven textiles and of decorative schemes derived from textile and basket patterns. A basket shown in a mural in Chichén Itzá's Temple of the Jaguars, for example, was highly elaborate in construction and decoration. Clothes represented in carvings on Classic Period Maya stelae, in the Bonampak murals, on painted Maya pots, in Aztec statuary and in painted codices give an idea of the range and quality of Mesoamerican woven materials.

Left: The musicians shown taking part in a procession at Bonampak wear elaborate headdresses and costumes.

FIGURES OF CLAY

Potters at Remojadas in the region of Veracruz produced very distinctive hollow clay figurines in the 8th–9th century (the late Classic Period). These craftsman, part of the 'Veracruz culture' associated with the city of El Tajín, were inheritors of an ancient Mesoamerican tradition. From as early as c.2500BC, at the beginning of settled village life in Mesoamerica, early craftsmen and women were making female figurines associated with cults of the land's fertility. One of these figures, dating from 2300BC, was found in a household fireplace at Zohapilco at the eastern end of Lake Chalco in the Valley of Mexico.

In the 2nd millennium BC, Olmec craftsmen made baby-face figurines called 'dolls' by some early archaeologists. These were beautifully produced hollow figures, with a surface coating of white, representing chubby figures with legs outspread and the face of a baby. The figures probably had some religious use associated with Olmec cults seemingly focused on the were-jaguar, a jaguar-faced human – often resembling a baby – thought by scholars to stand for the earth.

Olmec baby figurines were exported far and wide from centres such as La Venta and San Lorenzo using the Olmecs' extensive trading networks.

SHAMANIC RITES

About 1100BC, craftsmen made and used large numbers of handmade ceramic figures in the Valley of Mexico, in the villages of Tlatilco on the western side of Lake Texcoco and Tlapacoya beside Lake Chalco. Some were clearly used in association with shamanistic rites: they represented shaman-priests and weird two-headed creatures or three-eyed monsters that were perhaps the product of ecstatic visions and spirit-journeys following the consumption of mind-altering substances. Others were caught in such scenes of home life as mothers nursing babies or religious festivities

Above: This smiling boy (c.AD750–900) is typical of 'Remojadas figurines', with outstretched arms and wide, ecstatic grin.

and other celebrations involving cavorting acrobats, musicians and players of the sacred ball game.

Figurines such as this were produced in all parts of Mesoamerica in the Preclassic Period, but their use appears to have gradually died out towards the end of that era before reappearing in the mid-to-late Classic Period. Scholars have suggested that since the figurines were probably used in pre-temple religious rituals, they would not have been needed or welcome when formal religious life centred on temples became the norm. The new religious elite would probably

Left: These figurines made in Veracruz c.AD1200–1520 may represent ritual victims. The man (right) seems to be taking a hallucinogenic substance. Victims were drugged so that they seemed calm when going to their deaths.

have been keen to destroy all materials connected with rituals which they would have seen as outmoded. Archaeologists at Monte Albán, for example, report that hand-modelled figurines associated with household shrines disappeared from residential remains about the time that the building now called Mound X, identified as the city's first public temple, was

erected some time after c.300BC. It is unclear precisely how and under what conditions the practice of making and using figurines resurfaced.

STYLIZED TEOTIHUACÁN FIGURES

In Teotihuacán c.AD400, craftsmen used moulds to make articulated figures about 25–30cm (10–12in) in height. In stark contrast to the highly naturalistic representations of the later creators of the Veracruz Remojadas figurines, the Teotihuacános produced stylized figures with triangular-shaped faces, which generally have openings in the top of their heads. They also made non-moveable figures set in unusual postures. Scholars have not established a context in which these figures could have been used, beyond suggesting that they might have played a role in survivals of ancient village-based fertility celebrations in the wide spread of village communities around the metropolis of Teotihuacán. Then about AD650–700, Teotihuacáno craftsmen began to produce larger mould-made figurines representing nobles and deities on thrones.

RELIGIOUS ECSTASY

There was certainly significant Teotihuacáno influence in the Veracruz region, so the tradition of mould-made ceramic figurines in the great metropolis of highland Mexico might well have fed into the marvellous flowering of clay-figure moulding represented by the late Classic Period Remojadas craftsmen.

The gifted modellers at Remojadas made clay images of men, women and children, some attired as ball game players, some dressed as warriors. One distinctive form represented men – and more often women – with

Above: A Veracruz potter of c.AD500–950 fashioned this statue of a priest wearing a jaguar god headpiece and costume.

outstretched arms and elegant, wide-faced features, their mouths open and drawn in a broad smile or laugh, their teeth visible within their mouths.

The Remojadas potters produced highly naturalistic work. They decorated some figures with black asphalt paint to emphasize the features and details of the figures' often elaborate dress; other figurines they painted in many colours. Some scholars argue that the figures are in a state of religious ecstasy, having taken mind-altering substances. Others suggest that the laughing individuals are sacrificial victims whose unusual demeanour has been produced by swallowing hallucinogenic drinks intended to enable them to hide their terror and assume a joyful demeanour as they go to their deaths. The figures are typically about 30–45cm (12–18in) in height. The Toltecs at Tollán also produced mould-made clay figurines of people and animals, as did craftsmen at Xochicalco.

Left: Veracruz figurine c.AD250–500 represents a club-wielding warrior with skin blackened for battle.

187

MODELS FROM THE WESTERN ISLE

Maya potters developed great artistry in moulding clay figurines in the middle to late Classic Period (c.AD400–900). A large collection of exquisitely modelled figures was found in graves on the limestone Island of Jaina, just off the west coast of the Yucatán peninsula.

The island was a flourishing sea-trading and fishing centre for many centuries. In addition to its port and trade facilities, it contained two modest ceremonial centres named El Zacpool and Zayosal, together with a ball court and cemeteries in which the clay figurines were found. The buildings were simple, made of an earthen core that was faced with an irregular pattern of stones, then plastered with stucco and painted.

RULERS' GRAVEYARD?
Scholars are uncertain whether the splendid clay figures and wealthy grave offerings were laid in the tombs of rich local merchants, of priests and sacerdotal assistants at the ceremonial centre

Below: This kneeling figure, 15cm (6in) in height, is one of many Jaina Island models that represent ball players.

or of nobles and rulers from inland cities such as Uxmal and Kabah. Because the island's ceremonial buildings were modest, it would appear most likely that cemeteries were the graves of elite groups from the mainland rather than of locals. Jaina lay just off the coast and could be reached by foot through swamps at low tide. Because the island was on the western coast of the peninsula, the sun dropped behind it each night as it sank into the underworld Xibalba. Accordingly, some scholars argue that Jaina might have been chosen as the site for an elite cemetery because symbolically it lay on the path to the underworld.

Older figures found at Jaina, dating from before AD650, are generally solid and hand-modelled. After c.AD650, potters began to produce hollow figures made using moulds, perhaps in emulation of the Teotihaucáno craftsmen who were making hollow-mould figures from c.AD400–500 onwards. Some of the later Jaina artisans were not happy to rely solely on moulds and combined the new technique with older traditions producing, for example, a figurine with a mould-made torso but a handmade head. Many of the figures are musical instruments. Some, with holes bored in the back, are whistles. Others contained clay pellets and could be used as rattles.

PORTRAITS IN CLAY
The Jaina figures are generally 20–30cm (8–12in) tall. Some figures are highly naturalistic portraits – perhaps of the nobles in whose graves they were buried. They depict proud warriors with scarred or tattoed skins, wise old men, beautiful maidens and elderly matrons. Other statuettes represent less than idealized figures taken from life such

Below: The potters who made the Jaina Island models worked with great skill and delicacy, as evidenced in the attention to detail in the feather headdress, necklace, bracelets and ear decoration on this figurine.

188

Right: The Jaina Island tomb figures give us an invaluable insight into the clothes and headgear worn by Classic Period Maya.

as invalids, dwarfs, drunks and hunchbacks. One 7th–9th-century figure represents an old man who has lost his wits to drink. He holds a flask beneath his arm and has a look of unseeing stupefaction on his face.

Some of these models are careful representations of figures involved in religious ritual. One such 7th–9th-century figure represents a naked man with his hands tied behind his back, who would appear to be a noble prisoner bound for ritual sacrifice following capture during a war campaign launched by a rival city against his own. Another figurine depicts a ball player wearing protective belt and holding the ball prior to the start of a ball game. Other Jaina Island figures represent a shaman or priest in a trance.

IMAGES OF GODS

Some figures show gods and goddesses – usually divinities associated with the underworld. One such statue-pair from the 8th–9th century AD represents an elderly, lecherous man who is trying to raise the skirt of a beautiful maiden: scholars identify the man as a treacherous underworld lord and his consort as the moon goddess Ix Chel.

Another statue-pair represent a woman who is standing behind and over a seated male, almost enveloping him in her cloak. This may be a celebration of the protective power of Ix Chel in her role as mother goddess. A deity who is represented several times among the Jaina models is a figure called the Fat God, a squat full-faced man with a feathered headdress and very tall helmet.

The Jaina Island figurines were painted in bright colours. Curiously, the potters did not work hard on reproducing the feet or hands of their subjects, which were often finished without attention to detail, but they put great effort into reproducing individual physiognomies and styles of clothing as well as adornment with jewellery, headdresses and body art such as tattoos.

The figures have been an invaluable source for historians seeking information about details of Maya court life – such as elite clothing. The finest of the figurines are the older, solid ones made before *c.*AD650. Experts declare them to be among the finest pieces of their kind in all the Americas. Because so many of the figures were of warriors, some argue that the island cemetery might have been reserved for members of the military elite, or for rank and file members of the army who had won particular glory in battle.

Below: Scholars believe that this cloaked Jaina Island figure with mysterious headdress may represent an elite priest.

CERAMIC CULTURES

Fragments of pots, plates, bottles and jars generally provide the bulk of remains discovered by archaeologists when investigating living areas such as house platforms or household waste areas. In graves and temple offerings elite pottery forms are also well represented. The distribution of types of pottery and methods of decoration in different regions across spans of time gives a clue to the movements of people and influence. For this reason, archaeologists and historians often identify cultures by the type of pottery remains they left.

MANY-COLOURED SCENES OF COURT LIFE

The painted vases, plates, incense burners and drinking vessels produced in the Maya cities of *c.*AD550–800 in the late Classic Period were probably decorated by the highly educated noble artists usually referred to as scribes. Many of these vessels bore glyphic writing that gave the names and titles of the people represented and identified other elements of the image. Sometimes the glyphs provided an entire dynastic history for the ruler who was depicted sitting in state, conferring with his scribes and advisers, celebrating an anniversary of his accession or enjoying the chocolate drink.

EXPERT POTTERS

Some vases were incised with images and glyphs rather than painted, and in these cases the delicate lines were almost certainly cut by the same artists who were such skilled carvers of stelae and lintels.

We do not know whether specialist potters created the plates, cups and vases and then handed them over to be decorated

Below: Ceramics such as this painted vase from the Sula Valley, Honduras, accompanied elite burials in their tombs.

or whether the scribal artists were also responsible for making the pots. Some of the surface effects and colouring on painted vessels were achieved by expert manipulation of oxygen levels during the firing of the pottery and in these cases the scribal artists responsible for the final appearance of the vessel must have been involved in its firing.

Scholars believe that many of the scenes depicted on pictorial vases were taken from screenfold books. The scribal artists must have developed an expert judgement in order to transfer the elegant proportions of composition and neat glyph-work to the curved surface of the vase being worked.

There is very little evidence that the scribes first marked out the designs before painting over them, for this would have left visible marks beneath the final design. Scholar Michael Coe has suggested that the artists might have marked out the design in charcoal, which would have disappeared when the vessel was fired, but this can be no more than speculation.

Above: Deities were often shown in attendance at the scenes of religious ritual and court life represented on vases.

ROYAL FUNERAL RITES

Examples of elegantly painted Maya ceramics of the late Classic Period include the vessel known to archaeologists as the Altar Vase, found in the Usumacinta-region city of Altar de Sacrificios. According to scholar R.E.W. Adams, the image painted on the vase represents a funeral held in AD754 following the death of a royal woman of middle age.

Six dancing figures on the vase are believed to represent three visiting dignitaries from other cities, each accompanied by a *way* or spirit companion. The visitors, who had travelled from nearby Yaxchilán, from mighty Tikal and from an unidentified city in the highlands of the southern Maya region, laid offerings of fine ceramics in the royal tomb. The Altar Vase itself was laid in the grave of a young woman sacrificed in honour of the deceased princess or royal wife.

An image on the vase of a young woman performing rites of autosacrificial bloodletting might be a portrait of this young victim, who was herself probably a junior royal.

At Uaxactún archaeologists found a magnificent cache of painted ceramics in a stone tomb containing the corpse of an elite figure, probably a king. The corpse, buried in the building known as Structure A-I, was laid along the sanctified north–south axis used for ceremonial centres, with its head to the north. Next to the skull was a vase painted in the 8th century AD with a scene of court ritual using black and yellow against a red-orange base colour. The scene shows a king enthroned beneath a feathered shade held by an attendant. The king faces two elaborately dressed visitors, their visible skin painted black, one carrying a spear and one holding a ritual object with three spikes that scholars call a 'knuckle duster'. A seated jaguar, mouth open in a roar or snarl, accompanies the two visitors.

In all, the tomb contained eleven exquisite pottery pieces, nine of them painted. A beautifully painted tripod plate depicting a dancer had a small hole bored in it – the result of a ceremony performed to free the soul of the plate so that it could travel with the spirit of the deceased king as he made his way to the underworld. Many other delicately painted ceramics were left as grave offerings in Tikal, Seibal, Altun Ha, Tayasal and other settlements.

HIGHLAND VASES

Painted vases of very high quality were also produced in the highlands of the southern Maya region. A vase found at Chama in the valley of the river Chixoy, Guatemala, depicts seven individuals in red, brown and black against a pink base.

Right: Elaborately attired priests, warriors or gods ring a beautifully finished vase from Honduras, made c.AD600–900.

Two main figures face one another, both painted black, one wearing a jaguar skin. Individual features are represented in detail, suggesting that these were portraits executed from life. The black paint on the main figures might be intended to identify the two main figures as merchants by linking them to Ek Chuah, the patron god of that group.

Many vases, plates and cups were signed by the artists who painted them. For example, a cup for drinking chocolate was signed by Ah Maxam, the noble scribe from Naranjo who decorated it. The glyphs he inscribed in black paint on a cream base describe the function of the vessel and identify Ah Maxam as scribe and member of the royal household.

POTTERY FOR BANQUETS AND TEMPLES

México/Aztec potters specialized in a range of fired-clay braziers sanctified by the images of gods and goddesses. They were positioned outside temples or before the altars of the gods and used for burning aromatic copal incense, a form of rubber latex called *hulli* and body parts of animal and human sacrifices.

SMOKE GUIDE

The braziers were painted in bright colours. One splendid painted clay brazier of *c*.1500 found in Tlatelolco celebrated male and female vegetation deities Xiuhtecuhtli and Chalchiúhtlicue.

A set of five braziers of *c*.1500 commemorated warriors who had perished in battles or been sacrificed and whose souls were believed to accompany the sun god in his daily passage across the heavens.

Hulli was burned particularly in rituals honouring the rain god Tláloc, for worshippers believed that the dark smoke it produced would summon dark, rain-laden clouds. Some authorities taught that the smoke from ceremonial braziers could

Below: These elegant goblets are typical of the high-quality wares imported to Tenochtitlán from the Aztec empire.

lead the soul of a deceased person to the afterlife. Large braziers measuring 40–100cm (16–40in) or more in height were made to be placed on the ground, but smaller versions about 20cm (8in) long were threaded with cords through the handles and waved by priests to spread sweet-smelling copal incense around the temple.

Potters also made long-handled painted clay censers, with a round fretwork head that contained coals and incense. Priests waved the censer to perfume images of the gods and goddesses.

Potters produced goblets for use in temple rites. The sacred vessels were filled with blood and connected by straws called *pópotl* to the mouth cavities of god and goddess statues.

Two imported Mixtec goblets of *c*.1500, decorated with skulls and three painted bands (representing the night sky), were found in a burial cache of ceramics laid beneath an area of Tenochtitlán known as El Volador, thought to be the southern part of Moctezuma II's great palace.

Above: This lidded vessel decorated with images of the rain god Tláloc was made by potters in Tikal in the early Classic Period.

Aztec worshippers created a large demand for votive vessels decorated with images of gods and goddesses such as Tláloc, Chalchiúhtlicue, Chicomecóatl and Xilonen to be placed in temple offerings. Potters also produced clay plaques which were perhaps intended for temple display or for use as offerings. One, dating from *c*.1500 and found in Culhuacán, represented the rites of the festival of Ochpaniztli, in which a priestess of the maize goddesses Xilonen and Chicomecóatl wore the flayed skin of a sacrificial victim.

TINY TEMPLE PRECINCTS

Clay-modellers produced miniature temple structures, typically 30–40cm (12–16in) tall, for use in home shrines. They were detailed reproductions of Aztec Postclassic Period pyramid-temples, complete with balustraded stairways on all four sides of the pyramid, a sacrificial stone at the top of the steps and a simple temple building, perhaps with decorated roof. One of three such temples found in Calipan, modern Puebla state, was even painted with a red line down one stairway to represent the blood of sacrificial victims. The temples were probably placed on home shrines alongside small clay figures of corn, rain and fertility deities and used in rites linked to the festivals of the agricultural year. However, the temples were also used to honour other gods: the three models found in Calipan were made in honour of the fire god Xiuhtecuhtli, the earth mother goddess Toci and the war god Huitzilopochtli.

Potters in Puebla and Oaxaca specialized in large painted funerary urns with side handles. An important centre of production was the area known to historians as Mixtequilla Veracruzana in the south of modern Veracruz state where it borders Oaxaca.

These large vessels were also used to contain drink at ceremonial feasts. A mural at Cholula known as 'Los Belsilores' shows drinkers dipping their tankards into the large urn-like vessel. After being used in this way, they would probably have been placed in a temple offering.

Below: Small clay models of deities and of temple-pyramids were used in home worship until Aztec times.

Above: An architectural decoration representing a forerunner of Tláloc was made in Teotihuacán c.AD100–500.

BANQUET WARE

The ruler and nobles of Tenochtitlán imported their high-quality ceramics. Potters in Texcoco produced a polished red ware that was used by the nobility at banquets, to make offerings in the temple and to accompany high-ranking individuals in their graves. In Cholula and in Mixtec crafts centres in Oaxaca, potters produced polychrome ceramics that were also popular in Tenochtitlán.

Many examples of Texcocan polished red wares were put in tombs or survived. A splendid red-ware vessel with painted black designs now in the St Louis

Museum is typical of the style. Art historian John W. Nunley has interpreted the shell-like black markings as representations of the maguey cactus leaf and suggests that the vessel was intended for serving the alcoholic drink *pulque*, which was made from the fermented sap of the maguey. He adds that the phallic outline of the vessel's spout was intended to emphasize and celebrate the drink's reputed qualities as an aphrodisiac.

The nobles favoured painted tripod plates with elegant decoration in many colours. The legs of the plate often represented snakes, eagle heads or jaguar claws. A delicate cup made *c.*1500 for noble enjoyment was fashioned in the likeness of a flower, its long stem like four intertwining flower stems, and its bowl in the shape of a cluster of petals. Flowers were associated with the noble life: *pipiltin* nobility routinely held small bouquets of flowers to enjoy their scent and keep troubling smells at bay.

TENOCHTITLÁN'S LIFE-SIZE CERAMIC FIGURES

Aztec craftsmen produced remarkable fired-clay statues about 1.7m (5ft 4in) tall for the House of Eagles, a sacred precinct north of the Templo Mayor in Tenochtitlán. This was a notable development of the Mesoamerican tradition of making small clay figurines for use in worship. Aztec potters also followed this more modest path, making figures of deities such as Xipe Totec, perhaps 20cm (8in) tall. for use in domestic religious ritual and in temple offerings.

SUN COMPANIONS

A pair of life-sized statues representing eagle-warriors were mounted on a bench in the House of Eagles, which was used for penitential retreats and rites of autosacrificial bloodletting in which worshippers cut ears, cheeks or penis to offer blood to the gods. The statues were originally covered with stucco and decorated with a design in white paint that reproduced the eagle feathers worn into battle by these elite warriors. Each statue was made in four segments – the head and helmet; the torso and arms; the groin; and the lower legs. Archaeologists report that the eagle-warrior statues might have been images of the sun at dawn.

LORD OF THE UNDERWORLD

The House of Eagles also contained a pair of statues of Mictlantecuhtli, lord of the Aztec underworld Mictlán, also mounted on benches. One of the statues – 1.76m (5ft 7in) tall and 80cm (2ft 10in) wide – represented the hideous form of Mictlantecuhtli as a near-naked man with decaying flesh, bony torso and protruding liver, wearing a meagre loincloth, his hands vast claws, his mouth a terrifying grimace. Holes in the statue's skull would have held the dark curly hair associated with Aztec earth and death deities. Like those of the eagle-warriors, the statue was made in five pieces.

SKINNING OF THE MEN

Like their counterparts elsewhere in Mesoamerica during the Postclassic Period, Aztec craftsmen generally made smaller ceramic pieces using moulds. Four

Left: One of a pair of ceramic figures (c.1480) of underworld god Mictlantecuhtli, shown with exposed liver and grimacing mouth. Traces of the original white stucco covering are still visible. Like the warrior figure, above right, he stood in the House of Eagles in Tenochtitlán's sacred precinct. Here he stands on a tzompantli *(skull altar).*

Above: One of two life-size ceramic figures of eagle-warriors who stood in the House of Eagles, this was made c.1440–69.

figures found in Tlatelolco in 1968 celebrated the gruesome rites of the festival of Tlacaxipehualiztli ('Skinning of the Men') held to honour Xipe Totec, god of vegetation and germinating seeds.

The clay statues, each about 15cm (6in) high, represented priests and worshippers. Two warriors were seated on a bench, while two priests or other participants wore the skins of flayed sacrificial victims. An intermediate-sized statue, 97cm (3ft 2in) tall, of a Xipe Totec priest wearing the puckered skin of a victim was found in 1975 in the fortified city of Tepeji el Viejo in the mountainous southern part of modern Puebla state. The sacrificial statue, which was very beautifully made, had in its turn been sacrificed by being smashed. Archaeologists have reassembled the pieces to recreate the work.

BASKETWORK, MATS AND FURNITURE

The lakeside reedbeds of Mexico and Guatemala kept Mesoamerican basket-workers well supplied with raw materials. The makers of baskets and reed mats were practitioners of an ancient craft tradition and users of skills developed thousands of years earlier. Archaeological evidence shows that even before the beginnings of village life in Mesoamerica, hunter-gatherer groups made baskets, mats and sandals from reeds. In the Classic and Postclassic Periods, most working householders probably knew enough about reed-weaving to make their own simple mats and baskets for everyday use, just as they had sufficient rudimentary pottery skills to make their own pots, plates and cups.

Above: A detail from the list of Aztec tribute due from Tlatelolco to Tenochtitlán shows woven baskets of cacao and chia.

NAPATECUHTLI, PATRON GOD OF REED WEAVERS

The Aztec reed-weavers' patron god, Napatecuhtli, was represented wearing a tall headdress crowned with a *quetzalmiahuayo* ('gathering of sacred quetzal feathers'). A band of the bark paper used to soak up blood in rites of autosacrifice was wound around his head, with bark-paper ornaments suspended from it.

Doubtless because reed-weavers gathered their raw materials at the lakeside, Napatecuhtli was also a god of water and was associated with the rain deity Tláloc. For this reason Napatecuhtli's face was generally covered with a serpentine Tláloc mask, in which curling snakes formed eyes and upper lip. His robes were also made of bark paper and hung to his feet. He carried a reed sceptre or *oztopilli* in his left hand and sinuous snake-staff in his right hand. A delicately rendered fired-clay vessel of *c.*1500 representing Napatecuhtli was discovered in 1996 in Tláhuac, Mexico Federal District.

Specialist basket-makers made and supplied finer quality goods to those who could afford to barter for them at market. In the Aztec era, the reed-workers also made use of palm leaf, slats of cane and the leaves of the maguey cactus. They fashioned baskets in many sizes and shapes that could be used on *chinampa* fields, in the marketplace, in the household and even in the temple precincts for moving goods, storing food, secreting valuables or ritual items and keeping clothes away from dust and dirt. Other reed-weavers made *petlatl* mats and seats in fine weave for supply to nobles. Seats and low tables were generally restricted to wealthy households, while other folk used mats on the ground.

MAYA MATS AND BASKETS

The Maya of the Classic Period certainly used mats and baskets, but none has survived. An image of a basket carved on Lintel 24 in the city of Yaxchilán reveals how intricate Maya baskets could be. It combines three decorative schemes – a featherwork pattern, a twill design and a combination of frets and small squares – in a single item. The imprint of a Postclassic Period mat has been found on the floor of the shrine discovered beneath the Temple of the Feathered Serpent at Chichén Itzá. The pattern of its weaving is the same as that of mats still produced in the locality.

Mats were conceptually associated with political power. In Aztec society the *tlatoani* was known as 'the one who takes this place upon the mat'. For the Maya, too, the mat was the locus of authority. The title *ahpop* assumed by Maya rulers meant 'the one who sits on the mat'.

Below: A typically wide-eyed and grimacing Veracruz clay figurine of c.AD600–800 holds a woven basket full of produce.

RICHLY DECORATED ROBES

From sculptures such as door lintels and stelae we know that the rulers and noble elite of Classic Period Maya cities wore cotton fabrics with a rich weave and elaborate embroidery. Weavers made large amounts of cotton cloth in a variety of patterns. Only a few fragments of cloth produced by the ancient Maya have survived. A cache of chipped flints buried in the 6th–7th century Copán temple known to archaeologists as the Rosalila structure was wrapped in disintegrating fabric. A few pieces of white cotton cloth were discovered with late Postclassic pottery of *c.*1250–1500 at Tenam, a site in the eastern part of Chiapas. When archaeologists dredged the *Cenote* of Sacrifice

Below: Toltec warriors wore quilted cotton battle dress. This stone soldier, carved at Tollán, reproduces the costume in detail.

at Chichén Itzá, they found among the multitude of gold, silver and other precious offerings a few pieces of carbonized fabric with complex weaves.

AZTEC DESIGNS

In the Aztec empire, as in Maya lands, few pieces of cloth survived, but images in codices, in sculptures and in ceramics – together with the descriptions of Spanish invaders – reveal the rich variety of cloth and elegant decorative designs that were available.

As among the Maya, there were regionally distinctive designs. These were generally embroidered, woven, dyed or even painted on to the cloth. They were usually geometric designs, although some regions specialized in decorating with images of local animals or plants. The empire's finest textiles were those

Above: Used by Zapotec artisans, these loom shuttles carved from bones of the regal jaguar were placed in Monte Albán Tomb 7.

imported to Tenochtitlán from Veracruz. Huaxtec weavers, who were based in that region, produced highly prized white cotton cloth decorated with animal motifs.

Weavers made dyes from minerals, plants and animals. Red came from cochineal insects gathered in groves of nopal cacti – a useful sideline for agriculturalists. Blue clay and yellow ochre were other sources.

Purple came from the sea snail *Purpura patula*, found around the shores of Yucatán (see box). This snail was related to the Murex mollusc, found in the Mediterranean, from which the ancient Phoenicians made the 'royal purple' dye in classical Europe.

MAYA COLOUR CODE

Highland communities in modern Guatemala still follow ancient traditions in weaving practice, as far as historians can tell. These communities use handlooms to make cotton cloth and embroider this with cotton thread that has been dyed the required colour. Different communities have traditional designs. No two designs are identical, but they adhere to distinctive local patterns closely enough to be immediately recognizable. The meaning of the colours used also follows time-honoured ways. Red stands for blood, and blue sacrifice. Green-turquoise, the colour of the quetzal bird's magnificent tail plumes, is symbolic of royalty. Yellow, as the colour of maize, suggests food, while black stands for weapons – because it was the predominant colour of the obsidian used to make cutting blades for weapons. A deep purple colour derived from the sea snail *Purpura patula* found on the Pacific coast and carried inland by traders was highly esteemed.

COLOURFUL BATTLE DRESS

A celebrated portrait in the 16th-century manuscript *Codex Ixtlilxochitl* of Netzahualcóyotl, ruler of Texcoco, shows the colourful costumes available to the noble elite in Aztec Mexico. The portrait shows Netzahualcóyotl in ceremonial battle garb, bearing a blue shield, with long red tassels, on his left arm and on his head a blue headdress with white and red horizontal bands. These colours were matched in the blue of his tunic and the red of the protective binding on his upper arms. On his lower half he wears a flowing kilt in horizontal colour bands of white, red, green, yellow, red and green once more.

A page from the *Codex Mendoza* (c.1541) also made clear the bright colours worn by elite warriors for ceremonial dress. It depicts a selection of colourful outfits with elaborate feather headdresses and coloured shields decorated by *amanteca* feather workers.

Below: A modern Mexican hooked rug uses an Aztec design, incorporating images of birds and animals, and plant motifs.

FESTIVAL COSTUME

Clothes played an important role in religious ceremonies. At festivals, priests and priestesses, prisoner-sacrificial victims or commoners selected for sacrifice wore costumes that identified them as the god or goddess being honoured.

The costumes were often elaborate and highly coloured and so added to the spectacle and drama generated by these

Above: In August 2000, archaeologists excavating the Templo Mayor found this Aztec cloth in an offering to Tláloc.

public enactments of religious ritual. Colours and design elements added layers of religious meaning, a process well suited to representations of deities with many complex attributes, several of which they might share with other gods and goddesses.

For example, a celebrated statue of water goddess Chalchiúhtlicue (dated c.1500) found in Mexico City in 1824 wore the headdress that identified her as Chalchiúhtlicue, while her cape was embroidered with *chalchiuhtil* or jade symbols that were also essential elements of the goddess's outfit. However, she also wore a rattlesnake sash to hold up her lower garments and these associated her with maize goddesses and also with the earth goddess Coatlícue.

Statues like this one of Chalchiúhtlicue might have represented a deity or a priest/priestess impersonating a deity and showed details of festival dress. A few statues are naked or barely dressed figures and might have been dressed in brightly coloured real clothes as part of festival rites.

A GATHERING OF FEATHERS

Images in the *Florentine Codex* (1575–77) of Friar Bernardino de Sahagún depict highly skilled Aztec *amanteca* feather-workers at their job, sewing green quetzal feathers into elaborate headdresses for royal and priestly costumes, on to ceremonial shields and across temple banners. The emerald-green tail plumes of the male quetzal, gathered by specialist hunters in the tropical forests of Maya lands and imported to highland Mexico,

Below: Feather birds. These creatures on a painted terracotta brazier from Teotihuacán are stylized images of the sacred quetzal.

could be 1m (3ft 3in) long. It made a great visual impact when sewn around a headdress or added to its crown to make a tall *quetzalmiahuayo* (gathering of quetzal feathers). The feather-workers also used feathers from macaws, parrots, spoonbills and a range of other birds and made elite items of clothing, bracelets and magnificent costumes for dancing.

From at least the prime of Teotihuacán, in *c.*AD500, the transport of feathers was a major component of Mesoamerican trade. Other images in the *Florentine Codex* depict Aztec traders at market sitting alongside brightly coloured feather

displays. Feathers and feathered items were suitable offerings in temples because of their rarity and great worth. Quetzal feathers were additionally valued because of their length and, most importantly, because their colour resembled that of precious jade – the green of maize shoots and water, associated with Chalchiúhtlicue ('Mistress of the Jade Skirt'), and symbolic of life itself.

FEATHER-WORKING DEITY
The Aztec feather-workers, gathered in their own quarter of Tlatelolco, worshipped Coyotlinahual as their patron god. This deity was associated with Tezcatlipoca. In one version of the myth of Quetzalcóatl-Topiltzin as ruler of Tollán, when Tezcatlipoca arrived in the city of the Toltecs to bring about the fall of the Feathered Serpent through trickery and deception, he was accompanied by Coyotlinahual, who was identified as a magician.

EUROPEAN ADMIRATION
Feather-work was an unfamiliar craft to the Spanish invaders and one of the artistic achievements of the Aztecs and Maya that made the greatest impression on Europeans. (Although the conquistadors were keen to collect and send home Mixtec work in gold and silver, they admired it for its monetary rather than artistic worth and melted it down on its arrival in Europe.)

A magnificent example of the work of the most skilled *amanteca* was a *quetzalapanecayotl* ('quetzal-feather headdress') sent to King Charles V of Spain by Hernán Cortés in 1519 and now part of the collection of the Museum für Völkerkunde in Vienna, Austria. The vast headdress, which measures 1.16m by 1.75m (3ft 10in by 5ft 9in), contains 450 quetzal feathers adorned with gold appliqué and turquoise. It would have made a great impression, even from afar, when worn by priests of Quetzalcóatl in

Right: The Florentine Codex *depicts highly regarded* amanteca *craftsmen lavishing attention on a feather costume.*

processions and sacrificial rituals. Cortés collected a good number of featherwork items and sent a large consignment of them to Spain in 1522 but the precious cargo was seized by pirates.

NOBLE ADORNMENT

The Museum für Völkerkunde also contains a large fan, 1.19m tall and 68cm in diameter (3ft 10in by 2ft 2in), made from quetzal feathers and gold appliqué in the last years of the Aztec empire. Fans were used by rulers, nobles and elite *pochteca* merchants. These most elegant of Tenochtitlán's citizens provided a regular demand for the feathered fans produced by the *amanteca* of Tlatelolco. Nobles could be seen carrying a brightly coloured fan – feathered, for example, with the plumage of parakeets and hummingbirds – in one hand, and a bunch of flowers in the other. The fans were usually made with carved wooden handles.

Another fine survival of Aztec featherwork was a striking ceremonial shield, 70cm (2ft 3in) in diameter of *c.*1500, that depicted a creature some scholars identify as a long-tailed water beast called an *ahuítzotl* ('water-prickle creature'). Aztec legend had it that the *ahuítzotl* lay in wait for an unwary wanderer on riverbanks and lakesides, caught the wanderer in its tail and pulled him down to the depths of the water where he drowned. The beast's name was taken by the *tlatoani* Ahuítzotl (*r.* 1486–1502), who led vast sacrificial rituals for the dedication of the rebuilt Templo Mayor in Tenochtitlán in 1487.

Other historians have suggested that the beast on the shield is a coyote, an animal

Right: Amanteca *had many commissions from Tenochtitlán's religious hierarchy for feathered costumes worn in sacred ritual.*

form of the god Tezcatlipoca who was one of the patron deities of war, and that it might have been the mascot-symbol of an elite military order. The shield was made of reeds strengthened with lengths of wood and covered with animal hide. The craftsman stuck feathers of the spoonbill, oriole, macaw and cotinga to pieces of agave paper and glued these to the shield to create the design, adding quetzal plumes and more spoonbill and cotinga feathers around the rim. Strips of sheet gold emphasized the design.

MAYA FEATHERWORK

No examples of Maya feather-work have survived, but carved and painted images reveal the splendour of the capes, shields, headdresses, fans, spear pendants and other ornaments made by the Maya counterparts of the *amanteca*. At Piedras Negras, for example, Stela 12 depicts a ruler wearing both feather headdress and feather robe. Similarly, in Chichén Itzá's Temple of the Jaguars, wooden door lintels were carved with images of featherwork. The murals at Bonampak also provide evidence of elegant Maya featherwork designs.

IN THE CHRISTIAN ERA

The native craft of feather-work survived the Spanish Conquest, after which featherworkers' expertise in making priestly headdresses and costumes led to their contributing to the wardrobe and paraphernalia of Christian priests. The Bishop of Michoacán remarkable mitre was made in *c.*1530–60 from maguey paper and cotton cloth with a delicate mosaic of feathers from hummingbirds, macaws, parrots, cotingas, spoonbills, tzinitzans and starlings depicting events from Christ's Passion and the Last Judgement.

CHAPTER TEN

THE CARVER'S ART

The monumental carved heads of Olmec kings in the 2nd–1st millennium BC were raised in rows in plazas or ceremonial areas, where their steady, inscrutable gaze would fall on any who approached. Likewise the carved stone pillars or stelae of Maya cities in the Classic Period stood in great public spaces, a statement of dynastic power. Sculpture in Mesoamerica took two main forms: free-standing monuments, such as Olmec heads or Maya stelae, and decorative elements on buildings.

In many cases carving on buildings was also for public consumption – for instance, the stucco deity masks that flanked access stairs on Maya pyramid-temples and the dynastic scenes carved on temple roof combs were both visible from the plazas below. In other cases – such as carving on door lin-tels at Yaxchilán or Piedras Negras or on stucco panels within temples at Palenque – these carved elements were intended for viewing close up and would have been seen only by members of the priestly and ruling elite. They still celebrated divine blessing on royal achievement and consolidated the standing of the dynasty, but did so by what his-torians call 'horizontal propaganda' within a single social level as opposed to 'vertical propaganda' from a higher level (of the rulers) to a lower level (of the commoners).

Left: The Toltecs developed the coatepantli *or serpent wall. At Tollán, it limited access to the main ceremonial area.*

THE KING'S HEAD:
OLMEC MONUMENTAL CARVING

The craft of Olmec stonemasons appears to have burst fully formed into the history of Mesoamerican carving. Scholars know no precedent in the region for the monumental heads, three-dimensional figures, colossal royal thrones and early forms of stelae or pillars that the Olmec produced from the 2nd millennium BC onwards. The only three-dimensional representations in Mesoamerica before the rise of the Olmec in the Gulf Coast region were the small clay figures found at many sites including the villages around the lakes of the Valley of Mexico.

SYMBOLS OF ABSOLUTE POWER
Seventeen Olmec monumental heads have survived. They are remarkably similar, with fleshy faces and foreheads gathered in a frown. All wear a tight helmet or cap that comes down to just above the eyes. Some 2–3m tall (6ft 6in–10ft) and weighing up to 20 tons each, their size alone makes

Below: Scholars believe that the Olmec could identify individual kings or the dynasties to which they belonged by interpeting emblems in their head dresses.

them deeply compelling, but they are also arresting in their naturalism; in the lifelike detail of thick, slightly separated lips, the pupils of the eyes and the folds of flesh on the cheek. Simultaneously, their emotionless gaze makes them seem withdrawn and superior and is expressive of authority and absolute power.

MONUMENTAL FEAT
The heads were carved from large, smooth basalt boulders that occur naturally in the Tuxtla mountains around 80km (50 miles) from the Olmec temple towns of La Venta, San Lorenzo and Laguna de Los Cerros. The boulders were probably carved *in situ* in the mountains, then carefully wrapped and transported by river-raft to the ceremonial centres of these settlements, where hundreds of labourers assembled to move and erect the vast structures in rows.

Scholars believe that the heads were portraits in basalt of Olmec kings, perhaps the reigning lord or his most recently deceased ancestor, probably commissioned to mark funerals, coronation rites or important anniversaries of these

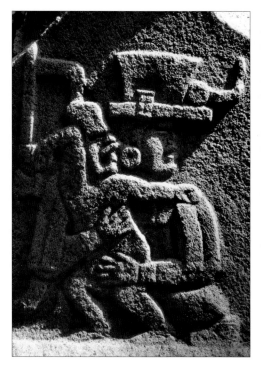

Above: La Venta Altar 5, marked with images of helmeted adults bearing 'were-jaguar' babies, was probably a royal throne.

Below: Olmec kings had power to deliver fertility, represented in this La Venta carving by the turtle shown above the ruler's head.

events. The headdresses are all different, marked with emblems that might have represented the king's name or that of the dynasty to which he belonged.

KNEELING BALL PLAYER?

Other notable Olmec stonework included a kneeling figure known as Monument 34 from San Lorenzo. Carved from basalt *c.*1100BC, the figure is 79cm (2ft 7in) high, with sockets cut at the shoulder that once held moveable arms and a carving of a concave mirror on his chest. Some scholars suggest that this kneeling male represents a player of the Mesoamerican ball game.

A statue carved at Laguna de Los Cerros *c.*1100BC is the only known standing figure carved by Olmec sculptors: the caped figure, nicknamed 'Superman' by scholars, stood 1.5m (5ft) tall.

More typical was a large greenstone statue of a seated man holding a baby that combined the features of a human infant with the square snout of a jaguar, an example of the 'were-jaguar' image commonly used by the Olmec and tentatively identified by scholars as an image of the rain god. This statue, found at Las Limas in Veracruz in 1965, is 55cm (22in) in height. On the knees and shoulders of the seated figure, the sculptor carved four profiled faces with distinctive features that may represent either four aspects of a deity or four distinct divinities.

Olmec craftsmen also carved several large stone thrones, which were once believed by archaeologists to be altars used in sacred ritual. Of these thrones, the most celebrated is the La Venta monument, which is known to archaeologists as Altar 4. This depicts a seated ruler in a bird headdress emerging from an opening in the front of the throne, holding a rope that connects him to a bound figure on one side of the stone. The same rope probably originally connected him to another figure on the other side, but this carving has been defaced. The

rope might indicate that the king had taken the other figure captive, or that the two were bound by dynastic links.

Archaeologist David Grove identified a buck-toothed ruler portrayed on Head 4 at La Venta as one of the bound figures represented on a throne at San Lorenzo. This suggests either that the two sacred towns had been at war and that a San Lorenzo king had captured a La Venta king, or that the monument celebrated

the kinship ties between the two ruling dynasties. On the La Venta Altar 4, a gaping jaguar's mouth was carved above the king suggesting that, in emerging from the niche in the stone, the king was coming forth from the heart of this regal predator.

Below: The posture and hand positions of this Olmec volcanic-stone statue led scholars to label him the 'standard bearer'.

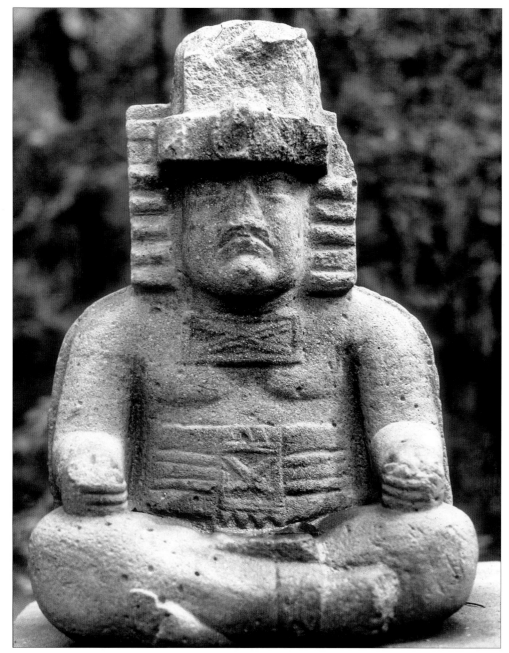

FROM THREE TO TWO DIMENSIONS:
THE FIRST STELAE

After *c*.500BC, Mesoamerican craftsmen moved away from the three-dimensional carvings of heads and seated or kneeling figures produced by Olmec artisans to concentrate largely on relief carvings in two dimensions. For more than 1,000 years, although potters continued to make clay figurines, relief carvings on panels, and thrones, slabs attached to buildings and stone pillars or stelae were the norm.

From the 6th century AD onwards, sculptors at the Maya city of Toniná created an unusual group of stelae that were carved on all four sides of the block, almost like a statue. Then in the 9th century AD, with the rise of the Toltecs – and perhaps in the Chalcihuites culture of northern Mexico, which some scholars now identify as a source of many Toltec practices and motifs – craftsmen returned to making this kind of monumental three-dimensional statue.

The Toltec-Maya at Chichén Itzá and the Aztec inheritors of Toltec power at Tenochtitlán were also enthusiastic practitioners of three-dimensional sculpture.

Below: The skeletal figure on this late Preclassic stone fragment from Izapa represents the underworld god of the dead.

Above: The deep relief carving of King Curl Head on Stela 10 (c.AD527) from Tikal has been eroded by time. Stela 10 stood on the North Terrace facing the Great Plaza.

CHALCATZINGO CARVINGS
The Olmecs had already demonstrated a great capacity for relief carving, evidenced in their high-relief work on stone thrones, in rock carvings and also in stone pillars or stelae. As early as 1100BC, craftsmen who were themselves Olmecs or who were working in the Olmec style cut elaborate reliefs in rocks at the trading centre of Chalcatzingo in the Amatzinac valley, to the south-east of the Valley of Mexico. One, dubbed 'El Rey' by historians, represents a king wearing an elaborate headdress, seated on a throne and holding a bar bearing a scroll design identical to the one carved on his throne, within a monster-mouth or cave believed to represent the entrance to the underworld. Art historian Esther Pasztory notes that the focus is on the importance of costume, equipment and location, as distinct from the monumental heads, which celebrated the power of the physical form.

Above: Some Monte Albán stelae celebrated the achievements of individual rulers. They were carved with dates believed to be birth-dates taken by the kings as their names.

Olmec stelae similarly celebrated rulers in elaborate costume. The monument labelled Stela 2 at La Venta, for example, represents a figure in ceremonial attire apparently holding a sceptre, weapon or bat. Historians suggest that the image may depict a player of the ball game – perhaps a royal ball game player. The stela, 2.46m (8ft) tall, was carved *c*.1100BC.

RECORDING THE CYCLES OF TIME
The Olmecs' contemporaries in Oaxaca also excelled at relief carving. At San José Mogote, Zapotec craftsmen carved a stone slab representing a fallen figure and set it in the doorway of a ceremonial building where people would tread. In the carving, known to archaeologists as Monument 3, skilled and learned stonemasons cut the day sign 1-Earthquake from the 260-day ritual calendar between the feet of the figure, perhaps to record the name of the person represented or the date on

Above: Danzantes. Some 300 carvings of ritual victims or prisoners – once thought to be dancers – were displayed on Building J as a statement of Monte Albán's might.

which he was killed or sacrificed. Cut *c*.700–500BC, this is the oldest evidence we have for the use of the 260-day calendar in Mesoamerica.

Shortly afterwards, in *c*.500–200BC, Zapotec artisans at nearby Monte Albán carved loose-limbed figures on the structure now called Building L or the Temple of the Danzantes. Slabs bearing these carvings were probably arranged along the side of the building. The fluid carving of these figures – believed to be prisoners of war or sacrificial victims – includes scrolls emanating from the groin, probably representing the flow of sacrificial blood after the priests had mutilated the victims' sexual organs, or possibly celebrating rites of autosacrifice in which the depicted figures had cut their

own sexual organs to offer their blood. Scholars note that the stonemasons here represented victims rather than rulers, and as at San José Mogote, exhibited a concern with marking the place of the images within the cycles of time.

STELAE IN MAYA LANDS

At Izapa on the Pacific coastal plain of Chiapas, in the southern Maya region, craftsmen developed a highly influential style in carving stelae from *c*.300BC onwards. They cut images of scenes from religious narratives, in which human-animal figures interact in making offerings.

Scholars identify Stela 21 at Izapa (cut *c*.100BC–AD100) as the first representation in Mesoamerican carving of the act of sacrifice. The pillar depicts a standing figure holding the head of a newly decapitated victim, whose lifeblood pours forth in long scrolls both from the head and the prostrate body, while in the background

a ruler or noble passes by in a sedan chair carried by two porters. Another roughly contemporary stela, number 25, represents a man or hero from religious narrative standing on the ritually important right-hand side of a scene, holding a staff on which a magnificent bird perches and facing a crocodile with its nose in the ground and tail vertically in the air. The stone-carver gave the crocodile an explicit likeness to a tree and indeed added a bird in the 'branches' of its tail. Scholars cannot fully explain the scene, but the crocodile, normally an image for the earth, may be a representation of the ceiba cosmic tree connecting underworld and heavens through the terrestrial plane.

Craftsmen also cut stelae in this period at Kaminaljuyú in the Guatemala valley. They carved rulers, generally portrayed walking in profile wearing elaborate garb and headdress and holding objects of ceremonial or ritual significance.

205

SET IN STONE:
THE POWER OF MAYA KINGS

Craftsmen in settlements such as Izapa, Kaminaljuyú and Abaj Takalik in the southern Maya region were cutting glyphic inscriptions that probably included calendrical dates in the years *c.* 100BC–AD250 (the late Preclassic Period). Fragments of what might originally have been dated monuments survive, but none of the dates themselves have been found.

CHANGING PERSPECTIVE

In these early years, Maya sculptors represented rulers with feet, legs and head in profile, but the torso turned towards the viewer with both arms visible. At Tikal, sculptors began to experiment with the position of the figure. Stela 4, dated AD378 and recording the accession of King Curl Nose, is the oldest known pillar to show a figure turned entirely towards the viewer. Another Curl Nose monument, Stela 18 of AD396, is the oldest known Maya image of a seated figure facing the viewer. Another early carving of a figure looking straight out of the pillar, Stela 26 at Uaxactún, is dated AD445. This position was then found on stelae throughout the Classic Period, at sites including Palenque, Yaxchilán, Piedras Negras and Seibal.

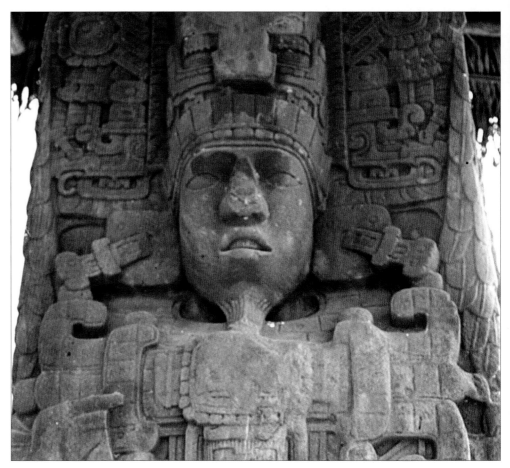

Above: At Quiriguá, Stela D is one of several in the Main Plaza bearing the face of King Cauac Sky (r. 724–84).

Below: Intricate Puuc-style carving surrounds a standing figure of the king on this monument from Kabah in Yucatán.

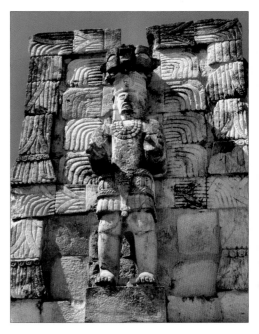

KINGS AND QUEENS OF CALAKMUL

The city of Calakmul, in south-eastern Campeche, contains 113 stelae – more than at any other Maya city. Some of these are unique in the Maya world in that they were raised in pairs that bear male and female portraits, understood to be the king and his queen. The first of these paired portraits were Stela 29 and Stela 28, raised by the city's second king in AD623. Another set, Stela 24 and Stela 23, were erected in AD702 by Calakmul's fifth king on the western edge of the city's Central Plaza.

Four stelae at Piedras Negras depict a newly inaugurated king in the position adopted on the celebrated Olmec Altar 4: seated cross-legged in a recess, facing the viewer. These four stelae were Stela 25 (dedicated in AD608), Stela 6 (AD687), Stela 11 (AD731) and Stela 14 (AD761). Each was an advance on its predecessor in terms of the success with which the carving was achieved, using progressively deeper recesses that permitted fuller development of the seated figure.

DEEP RELIEF

Images of kings facing out of the stela were most successfully developed by craftsmen at Copán and Quiriguá. At Copán, the carving on Stelae H (AD730)

ALL-ROUND CARVING AT TONINÁ

The stelae at Toniná, a city 50km (30 miles) south of Palenque, were unique in the Maya world in that they were carved in the round like statues. They were also unusually small, about 2m (6ft 6in) tall rather than the average for Maya stelae of 2.5–3m (8–10ft). Another carved structure at Toniná, known as Monument 122, features more conventional carving. It bears an image of King Kan Xul II of Palenque as a captive. Toniná's third ruler, who acceded to the throne in AD688, achieved a great coup in capturing Kan Xul II in AD711. Art historian Linda Schele suggests part of the tribute involved the despatch to Toniná of an elite sculptor from Palenque who was forced to carve an image of his defeated king.

Below: Many believe the deep-relief carving on Copán stelae to be the finest in the Maya world. Animal masks and complex regalia contrast with the serenity of the face.

Above: Quiriguá. The image of Cauac Sky on Stela E – which stands 10.7m (35ft) tall – is more than three times life size.

and Stela A (AD731) is extremely ornate and in very deep relief. At Quiriguá, Monument 5 (also known as Stela E and dated AD771) bears a splendid high-relief portrait of King Cauac Sky commemorating his victory over Copán. The largest known Maya stela, it measures 1.5m (5ft) wide by 10.7m (35ft) high and has an estimated weight of 65 tons.

CARVING THE GODS

Sculptors at Quiriguá moved on from stelae to carve large, unquarried sandstone boulders, subsequently known as zoomorphs, with images of sky divinities, earth creatures and kings.

One of these, Zoomorph P (also known as Monument 16), depicts a young ruler seated in the open jaws of a serpent representing the underworld and holds a shield with a sun god portrait and a sceptre of rulership. More than 3.4m (11ft) wide and 2.1m (7ft) high, the vast structure was typical of Maya sculptural aesthetics in its combination of natural and grotesque supernatural figures and the refusal to leave any space plain. The zoomorph was dedicated in AD795 and might have been cut to celebrate the accession of King Jade Sky.

THE WORK OF MAYA STONEMASONS

Maya carvers worked the rock that was locally available. For most this was limestone. At Quiriguá, Altar de Sacrificios, Toniná and a few other sites, stonemasons had access to sandstone, while at Copán they used a volcanic rock called trachyte. With a fine grain and predictable texture, trachyte was easy to carve and its availability at Copán was one important reason why that site rose to such prominence as a centre of the sculptor's art. The only drawback of trachyte was that it sometimes contained very hard flint

THE RULER'S ORNATE SCEPTRE
Maya kings were often represented on stelae and in other carvings holding 'the manikin sceptre', an ornately decorated staff symbolic of royal power: an example can be seen on Monument 16 at Quiriguá (carved in 795). Some centuries earlier, the influence of Teotihuacán on Maya sites had been seen in part by the carving of a Teotihuacano-style weapon, the spear thrower, on royal images: Stela 4 at Tikal celebrated the accession of King Curl Nose in 378 by depicting the king holding a spear thrower on his left arm beneath an image of the divine Maya patron of royalty, Bolon Tza'cab. Scholar Clemency Coggins demonstrated that the manikin sceptre symbol was formed by combining an image of Bolon Tza'cab with a carving of a spear thrower.

Above: Manikin sceptre.

lumps. These were either hacked off, creating small depressions in the monument's surface, or left in place, forming small lumps. Elsewhere, stonecutters needed to work limestone and sandstone shortly after it had been quarried, for the rock was soft when first exposed but grew harder the longer it was in contact with the air.

ANCIENT QUARRYING
Labourers quarried rock by digging along the sides and ends of an oblong shaft of stone suitable for a stela. Then, probably using tree trunks as rollers and creepers as ropes, they hauled the shaft to the site where it was to be erected. There they dug a receiving hole and lined it with masonry, then pulled the shaft upright into the hole, probably by building a ramp of logs behind the shaft and using an A-frame fashioned from wooden beams to raise it. Once the shaft was in place, they built platforms around it on which skilled carvers set to work. They used round-handled, single-edged stone chisels 5–15cm (2–6in) and hammer stones up to 7cm (2¾in) across.

After the carvers were finished, their work was rubbed smooth using sand and water, then plastered and painted. Most stelae were painted a dark red or blue mixed with copal resin. This produced a long-lasting coating with a varnish-like finish. In some places, particularly where the relief carving was deeper, the paint remains visible, more than 1,000 years later.

WALL PANELS AND LINTELS
In addition to stelae, Maya sculptors excelled in cutting wall panels, thrones, stone lintels and decorative elements on buildings. Some of the finest examples of wall panels and thrones were carved at Piedras Negras, roughly midway between Yaxchilán and Palenque on the river Usumacinta. A wall panel carved in the year 9.16.6.9.16 (AD757) adorned a nine-

Above: Serpent warrior. On the Temple of the Warriors at Chichén Itzá, a soldier emerges from the jaws of a sacred snake.

level mortuary monument now called Structure O-13 by archaeologists. The panel represents the fourth king of the Piedras Negras dynasty making a ritual designation of his son as the royal heir.

Below: This limestone chacmool, inlaid with shell and obsidian, was originally painted. He performed service as an offering stone for ritual victims' hearts at Chichén Itzá.

Above: Delicate limestone carving of courtly consultation adorned the back of a royal throne dated AD747 and found in Chiapas.

The king is depicted on his throne, with his son and two other boys standing on his left and three elite visitors from Yaxchilán, including King Bird Jaguar, on his right. Piedras Negras stonecarvers also created a magnificent, bench-like throne that was placed in the main room of the palace in a position where it could be seen by subjects standing in the courtyard before the palace. The stonemason-scribes carved glyphs on three sides of the throne's front legs; the inscriptions reveal that the piece was dedicated to royal use in 9.17.15.0.0. (AD785).

The finest carved stone lintels in the Maya world were the depictions of King Shield Jaguar and his wife Lady Xoc on Lintels 24, 25 and 26 at Yaxchilán. These images of Lady Xoc performing autosacrifice by drawing a thorn cord across her tongue, of Lady Xoc experiencing a vision and of the king dressing for battle ,were raised in Temple 23, dedicated to the queen and the gods in AD726.

At Copán, stonemasons excelled not only in carving stelae and altars or thrones, but also in providing elaborate decoration for architectural elements such as stairways and a platform with monumental stairway that archaeologists call a 'reviewing stand'. On the Hieroglyphic Stairway, which was dedicated in AD756, they cut more than 2,000 glyphs recording the city's dynastic history. The 63-step structure stood more than 20m (65ft) high and was 10m (33ft) wide, including its balustrades.

THE SEAT OF THE JAGUAR

In the 9th–10th centuries AD, rulers in the cities of the northern Maya region stopped commissioning carved monuments, instead employing stonecarvers to make decorative elements for sacred buildings. Artists at Uxmal produced an image of a head emerging from a serpent's jaws that was mounted in the façade of the base of the pyramid known as the House of the Magician. They also carved a new type of royal seat, the jaguar throne: a lifesized jaguar with flattened back on which the ruler sat. A jaguar throne has also been found at Chichén Itzá. Also at Chichén Itzá, under Toltec influence,

stonemasons carved the reclining *chacmool* figures that were set before temples. The arched figures each include a vessel into which the heart of a sacrificial victim was placed.

The carvers also made standard bearers, seated figures about 1m (3ft 4in) tall that held a feather banner, and the upright warriors that archaeologists now call 'Atlantean figures'. These were used to provide the support necessary for door lintels and daises.

Right: This standard bearer was made for the Temple of the Warriors in Chichén Itzá.

CHAPTER ELEVEN

PRECIOUS WORK

In April 1519 Moctezuma II sent magnificent gifts of gold and silver to Hernán Cortés and his conquistadors. The collection – which included a solid gold disc as big as a cartwheel, together with an even larger disc of silver – was intended to honour the newcomers and to impress the Aztec emperor's power and wealth upon them. The gift also made a religious statement, for the gold and silver discs represented the sun and moon and celebrated the pre-eminence of the Aztecs – self-styled 'People of the Sun'.

The Spaniards, versed in a different culture, could not be expected to understand the religious message: the gift served only to fan their lust for Aztec riches. Some members of the invading group, including Cortés himself, certainly admired the craftsmanship of the pieces – he wrote to Charles V about Aztec jewellery that 'nowhere in the world could a smith have done better'. But many Europeans could not see beyond the dazzling monetary value of the silver and gold; predictably, the discs did not survive – they were melted down for their metal, the fate that awaited the great majority of gold and silver ritual items, ceremonial jewellery and other pieces sent back to Europe by the conquistadors. Cortés despatched several loads of Aztec precious metalwork, and these were among the items that astonished German artist Albrecht Dürer, who declared them to be 'strange and wonderfully worked objects' that thrilled his heart.

Left: God of spring and goldsmiths. This exquisite gold mask of Xipe Totec was an offering in Tomb 7 at Monte Albán.

AN IMPORTED CRAFT:
METALWORK IN MESOAMERICA

On 6 January 1932 Mexican archaeologist Alfonso Caso made a breathtaking find in a tomb at the Zapotec mountaintop city of Monte Albán. The grave had originally been laid out *c*.AD 500–750 with a large fore chamber leading into two rooms aligned east–west. These contained a stone carved with Zapotec glyphs and a number of funerary urns. The grave had then been reopened in the late Postclassic Period (*c*.1250–1500) by local Mixtec mourners, who buried nine skeletons with a magnificent tribute-cache of metalwork and jewellery. The grave, known as Tomb Number 7, contained no fewer than 121 golden objects, 24 silver objects and a large number of rings, necklaces and pendants. This find provided ample evidence of the Mixtecs' astonishing skill in metalwork and making jewellery.

LATE STARTERS
When compared to their South American neighbours, Mesoamerican craftsmen were late starters in metalwork. Native Mesoamericans did not make jewellery, ritual items, weapons or tools from metal until after *c*.AD800. As early as 2000BC, the inhabitants of the Andes mountains in South America had begun to develop metalworking techniques that slowly travelled northwards along marine and land trade routes. These techniques took almost 3,000 years to reach Mesoamerica, probably arriving roughly simultaneously in two separate areas: the northern Maya region of the Yucatán peninsula and, hundreds of miles to the west, coastal settlements in western Mexico.

Among the oldest metal objects in Mesoamerica is a small claw, *c*.AD550 in Panama. It is made of the alloy of silver, copper and gold known as tumbaga, and was buried in the ceremonial centre of Altun Há, on the coastal plain north of modern Belize City. Later, a hollow figure of a gold-copper alloy was deposited as part of a cache of valuables beneath Stela H at Copán. The stela was dedicated in AD782, although archaeologists cannot rule out the possibility that the cache was buried after this or added to at a later date. Only the legs of the figurine remain, but expert analysis of the casting and alloy suggest that it was imported from a site in the southern parts of Central America such as Panama or Costa Rica.

BEGINNINGS IN MEXICO
Archaeologists have established that in the earliest days of Mesoamerican metalworking, during the 9th century, artisans working with copper in western Mexico were producing the same items in the same way as their counterparts in

Left: One of the finds in Tomb 7 was this Mixtec gold pectoral or breast ornament representing the 'old fire god' Xiuhtecuhtli.

Left: This Mixtec gold earring was one of the hoard buried in Tomb 7 at Monte Albán. The Mixtecs' exquisite gold jewellery and other fine metalwork was admired and highly influential across Mesoamerica.

Another metalworking centre was established at Amapa, Nayarit, about 50km (30 miles) inland from the Pacific coast, on the river Santiago. Here artisans made copper rings, knives, needles, pins, axe-heads, beads, plaques, bells and awls.

In Michoacán the Tarascans worked local copper to produce small ritual figures, tweezers, open rings, needles and a large numbers of bells. They also made copper axe-heads that were used as a form of money.

In Oaxaca the Mixtecs began developing their metalworking expertise after AD900. They became the pre-eminent metalworkers of the Aztec age, when some Mixtecs worked as producers of jewellery and precious-metal items in Tenochtitlán, while others worked in their own centres in Oaxaca. México/Aztec craftsmen centred in Azcapotzalco also produced metalwork in the Mixtec style. They worked in gold, silver and tumbaga.

In the northern Maya region, metal-workers developed great expertise in repoussé work, hammering designs into a sheet of metal from the reverse side. Many repoussé pieces hammered from both gold and copper were found among the objects cast into the *Cenote* of Sacrifice at Chichén Itzá. They depicted scenes of conflict between Maya soldiers and warriors of the invading wave of 'Mexicanized' merchants.

THE GODS' GOLD

Gold was identified as *teocuitlatl* ('the gods' excrement') in the Nahuatl tongue, probably because it was found in nuggets, like the droppings of animals. Its colour meant it was also associated with the sun. Images of the gods sometimes represented them wearing the gold jewellery worn by rulers, warriors, nobles and priests. A stone casket of the late 15th century that belonged to the *tlatoani* of Tenochtitlán, Ahuítzotl (*r.* 1486–1502), depicted the god Tláloc wearing a necklace carved with the symbol for gold. A statue of Xochipilli of *c.*1350–1500 shows the god of flowers and music wearing a gold necklace.

Below: This Mixtec painted vase is of a human head laden with jewellery with pierced earrings and an elaborate headdress.

Ecuador. They were making needles, rings, tweezers, fishhooks, axe-heads for wooden-handled weapons and the sharply pointed pricking instruments known as awls. There is evidence that smelting and metalwork were carried out on the coast of Guerrero by *c.*AD900. In a settlement at Zihuatanejo, archaeologists uncovered slag pieces (the refuse separated from metal when it is smelted) and many bronze and other metal pieces in a find dated *c.*AD900–1100. The metal pieces included rings, bells and sheets of gold.

CHIPPED AND CARVED STONES:
ELABORATE OFFERINGS

Maya artisans chipped and cut stones, blades and flints with elaborate skill. Obsidian and flint blades and the remarkable decorative chipped flints known by scholars as 'flint eccentrics' were sacred objects, buried in large caches beneath temples and monuments.

FLINT ECCENTRICS
Some eccentrics are fashioned to represent human heads in profile. A number of chipped flints found at El Palmar, Quintana Roo, were probably once the heads of ritual staffs. One represents a human figure, with elaborate headdress, protruding lips perhaps intended to suggest a lip plug and a large ornament on

Below: This carved Maya jade pendant, 12cm (5in) across (c.AD850–1250), was found in the Sacred Cenote at Chichén Itzá.

the back. The 6th-century Copán temple that archaeologists call the 'Rosalila structure' contained a large cache of chipped flints, including a number of human profiles. Scholars believe that these may once have been the heads of the 'manikin sceptres' carried by Maya rulers as a sign of authority. Other flints are chipped to represent leaves or the form of the symbols of office called 'knuckle dusters' by scholars and held by notable court attendants in murals and painted scenes on vases.

Above: An Olmec jade piece was carved in the form of a canoe c.500BC. Sacred markings are visible at the ends.

CARVED FIGURES AND PLAQUES
From the days of the Olmec, Mesoamerican craftsmen cut small pieces of jade and other stones with remarkable delicacy and precision. An Olmec jade bead found in Chiapas was fashioned in the shape of a human head, while another small jade found at Necaxa in modern

WORKING JADE
Technically, Maya jades are jadeite, a very hard mineral with a chemical composition distinct from that of nephrite, the material carved in Chinese jades.

Mesoamericans gathered jadeite from streams and rivers in the form of pebbles, rocks and even sizeable boulders. Skilled craftsmen used a sawing motion with cords to cut and deepen lines in the hard rock, drilling holes with bones or pieces of hardwood, in both cases using water and sand or tiny stones to aid in cutting. The precision, delicacy and artistic flair of their work is astonishing.

Partly because the rock was found in streams, but more significantly because of its typical mottled green to blue-green colouring, jadeite was associated with water and fertility among the Aztecs, and with water and rain deities such as Chalchiúhtlicue and Tláloc.

Above: An Olmec jade figurine, found at La Venta and made c.1200–200BC, is believed to represent the god of the maize plant.

Puebla state was cut in the shape of a crouching tiger. In Maya lands, archaeologists found several delicately carved figurines in jade and other similar stones during excavations at Copán, Chichén Itzá, Uaxactún and other sites.

The small, carved heads were often worn as pendants. One found at Chichén Itzá bore a date in the Maya Long Count equivalent to AD674. Scholars believe that traders brought it to Chichén Itzá from Piedras Negras, its probable place of origin. A cross-legged human figure beautifully fashioned from fuchsite, a stone similar to, but softer than jade, was deposited in an offering at Uaxactún beneath a stairway at the structure archaeologists call Temple A-XVIII. The figurine had linked forearms, rounded belly, rectangular eye sockets originally painted red and a large left ear – its right ear was apparently damaged. Holes drilled in the stone probably gave such ornamental pieces ritual meaning.

At Palenque, a carved jade figurine of the Maya sun god Kinich Ahau was placed within King Pacal's sarcophagus in the royal tomb beneath the Temple of the Inscriptions. A substantial jade head of the same god, found in a king's tomb at Altun Há in Belize, weighed 4.42kg (9.7lb), making it the largest Maya sculpture in this precious stone.

CELTS, PLAQUES AND PECTORALS

A 4th-century jade celt or implement, probably worn as a belt decoration, was carved with the Maya Long Count date 8.14.3.1.12 (17 September AD320) and with a full-length portrait of Tikal ruler Moon Zero Bird. The celt, known by scholars as the Leyden Plaque, celebrated Moon Zero Bird's 'seating' or accession to the throne of Tikal on the marked date in AD320. It depicts the king, in full ceremonial costume with celts and deity masks hanging from his belt, trampling on a captive depicted in a style similar to that used for images of captives on Tikal monuments. The plaque, one of the oldest dated Maya artefacts, was probably taken from King Moon Zero Bird's tomb at Tikal in ancient times. It was found in 1864 at Puerto de Barrios near the river Motagua in Guatemala.

A blue-green jade plaque, 30cm (12in) tall, was carved by a leading jade-craftsman of the late Classic Period Maya world. It represents a king on a throne, his body facing forwards but head in profile, wearing a serpent headdress from which emerges a figure with an unsettling, grotesque face. Before the throne a second figure kneels in supplication, while

Right: An Olmec adze, or type of axe, from Veracruz is carved with the features of the sacred jaguar.

a speech scroll coming forth from the king's mouth indicates that he is declaring his identity and mighty achievements or else offering prayers to the gods on behalf of his people. The beautifully worked piece, found in Teotihuacán, was perhaps offered as an elite gift or else traded for valuable goods.

A splendid jade pectoral cut by Mixtec craftsmen c.AD1000 bears witness to the continued popularity of this precious stone for ceremonial and sacred objects.

CHAPTER TWELVE

IMAGES, SYMBOLS AND WORDS

Mesoamerican wall paintings are filled with religious and political meaning. Sometimes accompanied by explanatory hieroglyphs, they are sacred statements, often dense with complex symbolism, intended to be 'read' and interpreted: celebrations of the gods' goodness in guaranteeing the fertility of the earth, of the power of the king and his ancestors or of the movements of time as evidenced by astronomical cycles.

Classic Period Maya-painted scenes include the humiliation or sacrifice of a defeated ruler, victory in battle, ceremonies of dynastic consolidation or acts of ritual bloodletting. Images represent action and carry narrative, while glyphs provide meaning and permanence by giving names and by setting the events in time.

In a parallel tradition, beginning in Teotihuacán and also finding expression in murals at Cacaxtla and in Caribbean Yucatán in the 13th–16th centuries, artists created symbolic religious scenes connected with the underworld, fertility and the cycles of the stars rather than dynastic or military events. In this tradition, glyphic writing played a much smaller role – there were no glyphic inscriptions at Teotihuacán. But scholars are convinced that religious symbols such as the five-pointed half-star Venus sign could be 'read' as part of a 'symbolic writing' by residents of Teotihuacán or Cacaxtla.

Left: Solar symbolism. A mural in Cacaxtla shows a man with eagle beak and wings who may represent the sun by day.

*Above: Divi[...]
were plotted [...]
modern reco[...]*

units of 20.[...]
number of u[...]
the number[...]
number of [...]
and the fo[...]
(20 units o[...]

A tall col[...]
Ambassad[...]
the Olmec[...]
historians [...]
evidence [...]
Some t[...]
500BC, ston[...]
of the colu[...]
bearded m[...]
ambassad[...]
(which app[...]
which, a b[...]
his calend[...]
carvers of [...]

T

GLYPHS AND IMAGES

The
patt
migh
Meso
syste
that
calen
form:
mid-

CYCI
As fai
first u
milita
the cy
The
piece
hieros
Monu
These
the 26
of a pi
The
identif
later M
from

Below:
the Pal
depicted

*Above: This cylindrical vase from Uaxactún
is marked with a symbol and date that may
record the owner's birth-date and name.*

Sculptors of Maya stelae embedded their meaning in the image. Viewers were expected to understand the hieroglyphs in conjunction with the image portrayed. The image could be of a king with his defeated rival or of a ruler performing sacred rites of bloodletting. The hieroglyphs placed the event in the cycles of time and named the protagonists.

TYPICAL INSCRIPTIONS

A typical stela inscription began with detailed calendrical information, giving the precise day on which the event celebrated in the image took place. First it named the patron god or goddess of the month, then it gave the Long Count date and transcribed this same date into the

*Above: Meaning in action. Divine rulers
and gods adopt abstract postures in Mixtec-
style codices. This page is from the* Codex
Zouche-Nuttall, *which may have been a
gift from Moctezuma II to Hernan Cortés.*

260-day ritual calendar, naming the god among the nine lords of the night who controlled that day and the phase of the moon that applied.

After this, an inscription might specify an event or anniversary of ritual significance that applied to the depicted activity, such as a *katun*-ending, then name the king and any other protagonist who had been involved.

Sometimes the glyphs giving the identity of the king would also name his ancestors or his offspring. At other times they would provide evidence of recent heroic activity. For example, various

glyphs identified the king as lord of five, ten or even twenty captives. Following glyphs might give dates for subsequent events such as the king's partaking in ritual bloodletting or sacrificial worship. The second date in an inscription would be given only in the 260-day calendar, since the historical context within the Long Count had already been established.

Above: The Maya used these glyphs to convey historical and dynastic information. From top left – 'was born'; 'acceded to throne'; 'event of taking captive'; 'taker of captives'; 'taken captive'; 'he'; 'she'; 'wife'; 'ruler's number in dynastic line'; 'king or queen died'.

NAMING

Some scholars liken the glyphs naming kings and dating their stelae to the name tags that the Maya inscribed on sacred and everyday items such as incised bones, ear ornaments and drinking vessels.

The practice of name-tagging was discovered by scholar Peter Mathews in 1979 when studying an ear flare from Altun Há, Belize. The ornament was inscribed with the phrase *u tup* ('this man's ear flare'), together with the name of the owner, who was a member of the royal family. Name tags were subsequently identified on incised bones from the tomb of King Ah Cacau in Tikal, and on plates, dishes and vases.

Scholar Michael Coe found a repeating pattern of hierogylphs on elaborately decorated polychrome vases of the late Classic Period. This pattern, named the Primary Standard Sequence, amounted to a formula for naming and dating vases.

Generally painted around the outer rim of the vase or bowl or sometimes placed in a vertical column, it included up to 22 glyphs, always in the same order, but often with some missing and sometimes with as few as three glyphs. The sequence begins with several initial glyphs, sometimes including the head of the god Pawahtún, a four-fold god of the directions. This is thought to have functioned as a dedication of the vessel. Then came glyphs indicating whether the pot was carved or painted and identifying its shape, its use (perhaps for drinking or serving cacao), its owner and the artist who produced it. Sometimes the sequence also includes a date in the Calendar Round, which unusually referred to the date the object was made rather than the date on which the depicted events took place.

WORDS IN CODICES

In codices and in murals – just as in the inscriptions on stelae, stone thrones, zoomorphs and ceramics – words functioned to identify names and provide calendrical information, while images represented the activity that was being celebrated. In such pre-Conquest Mixtec books as the *Codex Zouche-Nuttall* or the *Codex Cospi*, illustrations were not designed primarily for aesthetic effect but to convey meaning.

Glyphs generally identified three key facts: dates, places and names. The human figures took a limited number of stylized postures, usually walking, standing or seated in profile and deity figures were usually shown in a flat, full frontal position. There was no attempt to achieve the naturalistic effects found in Classic Period Maya murals, stucco-work and polychrome vases and in Postclassic statuary.

Below: The highly prized role of the scribe could be taken by royal or noble women as well as by top-ranking men. This Maya ceramic shows a female scribe at work.

THE AGE OF BOOKS

In the Postclassic Period, the artistic style of Mesoamerica derived largely from that of codices. Ceramic decorations, mural images, representations on monumental state sculpture and decorative symbols in jewellery are all similar to illustrations in the codices. Because the largest number of surviving codices were written and painted by Mixtec scribes working near the city of Puebla, scholars call this the 'Mixteca-Puebla style'.

The style was not regional but far-reaching and even international. In Tenochtitlán, images carved on state monuments resembled pages from a codex. In Oaxaca, delicate jewellery figures and fine murals at Mitla had the 'codex style'. On the Caribbean seaboard at sites such as Tulum in eastern Yucatán and Santa Rita Corozal in northern Belize, 15th-century murals closely mirrored the appearance of Mixtec codices.

SACRED SYMBOLS:
OLMEC AND TEOTUHUACÁNO MURALS AND FRESCOES

Finds of superb murals in the sacred city of Teotihuacán, in Maya cities such as Bonampak and in highland Mexican settlements such as Cacaxtla provide evidence of a highly developed Mesomerican wall-painting art.

TRADITION OF WALL-PAINTING
The roots of this tradition date all the way back to the Olmec period, when artists decorated sacred caves with distinctive ritual imagery. In caves in the southern Sierra Madre mountains, modern Guerrero province, historians have found cave paintings representing kings, a stone throne, sacred serpents and a fierce jaguar.

The oldest of these paintings are probably those at Juxtlahuaca and Cacahuaziziqui, which date to *c*.1000–700BC. One of the images at Juxtlahuaca represents two men, one seated and the second standing in elaborate costume that includes a hooped tunic-skirt, jaguar skin and black cloak, together with a feather helmet. The standing figure holds a

Below: Were mural painters in Teotihuacán using a language of nature symbols? This strange bird adorned a residential complex.

serpent-like object in his left hand, while his right controls a ritual implement – perhaps a sceptre or a sacred tool like the 'knuckle-duster' seen in later Maya paintings. Other Juxtlahuaca paintings represent a jaguar with black outline and

Above: Sacred animals in the Jaguar Palace (c.AD400) in Teotihuacán were intended to bring bounty to the city's inhabitants.

a red-bodied serpent with fiery eyebrow and the distinctively Olmec cross (like the cross of Saint Andrew) on its face. Two figures painted at Cacahuaziziqui appear to have glyphs close to their mouths, as if representing speech.

At Oxtotitlán, near the town of Acatlán, artists created an intriguing set of cave paintings *c*.800–500BC. A large image of a ruler seated on a throne dominates the sacred cave. He wears an owl mask and feathered cape, together with a skirt bearing the Olmec claw-wing symbol. His left hand reaches vertically up, his right hand reaches down diagonally, while his left leg is drawn up and his right leg falls down before him. His throne represents a monster mask with open jaws.

A second image depicts a man, painted in black outline with outstretched right arm, standing behind and possibly performing a sexual act with a fierce-faced jaguar. A third mural at Oxtotitlán shows a four-petalled flower with a human face at the centre. This is suggestive of later cosmological images that represent the universe as a flower with a petal to north, south, east and west and the tree of life in the centre.

TEOTIHUACÁN MURALS

Among the people of Teotihuacán were skilled potters, makers of haunting masks and magnificent monumental architects. However, mural painting was without doubt the art in which they most excelled.

Teotihuacános created wall paintings from *c.*AD300 onwards, first decorating small structures lining the Street of the Dead. After *c.*AD500 they began to paint murals in the city's many apartment compounds and in the palace areas close to the Pyramid of the Moon and the Pyramid of the Sun.

Their style was almost abstract. They painted few narrative scenes such as battle victories or rites of sacrifice and no naturalistic portraiture, but used a wealth of stylized images and motifs taken from nature, such as shells, stars, coyotes, and jaguars. In recent years, scholars have argued that Teotihuacáno artists used these religiously charged signs as a form of symbolic written communication.

The artists first prepared the walls by applying a layer of clay, later adding a coat of lime mixed with sand and quartz. Once the surface was ready, the painters set to work, first applying a red background colour then drawing designs in black and a darker red. They filled in additional colours of blue, green and yellow as the last stage in the process.

THE GREAT GODDESS

Many murals contain images of the Teotihuacános' supreme deity, dubbed the Great Goddess by art historian Esther Pasztory. Like many Mesoamerican divinities, the goddess had dual aspects as both a beneficent giver of life and as an awe-inspiring force of evil. She was recognizable from her red and yellow zigzag band, her nose bar and her bird headdress. The murals of the Tepantitla apartment building show the goddess in her lifegiving aspect in a river setting, with water creatures and abundant growths of flowers. In the Tetitla building, meanwhile, she is seen in her evil aspect, with fangs and bestial claws.

The goddess clearly possessed fertility aspects, but otherwise had little connection to other female deities of Mesoamerica – her cult was apparently unique to Teotihuacán. Other gods represented in the Teotihuacán murals have closer links to those of the wider Mesoamerican pantheon. One is the storm god, with strong links to lightning and thunder and to the god the Aztecs called Tláloc. Another is the feathered serpent god whom the Aztecs called Quetzalcóatl. A third, an aged god represented as a crouching man supporting a brazier on his skull, was later known to the Aztecs as Huehuetéotl.

THE TECHINANTITLA COMPOUND

These paintings, produced *c.*AD600–750, are unusual for Teotihuacán in representing scenes of military life. They include a long procession of figures wearing a tasselled headdress associated with warriors and positions of power. Above and below the figures, a border consists of footprints. Eight of the marching warriors have glyphs painted by them, probably representing their names. Another section represented trees.

Below: Water falls from the hands of an early version of the pan-Mesoamerican rain god in a mural from Teotihuacán.

SYMBOLISM AND NATURALISM

The artists of Teotihuacán produced representations in murals, pottery, masks and figurines that exhibited little interest in naturalism and far more in religious symbolism. Humans were anonymous members of a mass group: in masks, human features were often reduced almost to geometric shapes or hidden behind nose bars. Murals tended to represent people in profile, often in procession, moving towards a goddess or god figure who was shown full frontal. Many scenes were of animals, plants and deities, often involved in rites associated with fertility. These images did not glorify the military and political achievements of rulers, apparently focusing instead on deities and religious symbols.

In contrast, many Maya muralists, stucco sculptors and ceramicists of the Classic Period (AD250–900) excelled in naturalistic representations of the human face and body. At Bonampak, for example, the suffering of prostrate prisoners of war was depicted with deft and feeling naturalism in Room 2 of Temple 1. Images of court life on polychrome vases and stucco carvings of King Pacal or King Chan Bahlum at Palenque are accurate and fluid representations of human expressions and gestures. (This is distinct from the much more stylized representations of royal figures produced by stonemasons on stelae and stone thrones.)

Images in Maya murals, ceramics and stucco focused on the beauty of the human body and face and of ceremonial attire such as the headdresses and costumes that also glorified the gods through sacred symbolism. Artists celebrated an ideal of human beauty in the stucco heads of King Pacal at Palenque and in the young maize god at Copán; in images of kings and courtiers on polychrome vases and in murals. This ideal consisted of a serene face with wide eyes, the bridge of the nose built up to join the forehead, full lips and smooth cheeks.

ROYAL PORTRAIT CONVENTIONS

Maya muralists and other artists generally stayed within established conventions of representation. They usually showed royal figures as exemplars of ideal beauty, not prone to ageing, in elegant costume

Above: Stone beauty. Maya sculpture probably reached its apogée in work such as this elegant head found at Copán.

and standing formally or occupying a regal seat. Artists had more leeway when it came to scenes of battle or those involving prisoners. The muralists at Bonampak took full advantage in representing an intense battle and subsequent presentation of prisoners to King Chan Muan in Room 2 of Temple 1. They showed soldiers and prisoners in many lifelike postures and expressions, prone and sitting, striding and thrusting, grimacing with pain and rolling their heads as if about to lose consciousness.

THE SHAPE OF A KING

Artists at Palenque made a limited departure from the tradition of idealizing the physical appearance of the ruling family. Doubtless on royal orders, they appear to have emphasized physical abnormalities peculiar to the ruling dynasty of King

Below: Coiled force. One of many sculptures of the sacred serpent by Aztec artists illustrates the powerful naturalism they achieved.

Above: The artists who painted this mural in Tomb 105 at Monte Albán used symbolism reminiscent of Teotihuacán.

Pacal. These included an outsized head and jaw, signs of the pituitary disorder known as acromegaly, seen in images of Pacal's mother Lady Zac-Kuk. Depictions of Pacal's son, Chan-Bahlum, on the Temple of the Inscriptions show him with six fingers on the left hand and six toes on both feet. One of Pacal's uncles had a club foot, and scholars believe that Pacal himself might have inherited this. In images Pacal's foot was stylized as a serpent, and from the early 10th century AD, a god with serpent feet, Bolon Dz'Acab, became established as patron of kings. King Chan Bahlum appears to have encouraged his sculptors and artists to pursue a more realistic style in portraiture, as evidenced by a portrait head of the king in Temple XIV which depicts him with natural features at odds with the Maya ideal.

These dual strands of Maya naturalism and Teotihuacáno symbolic art had a joint flowering in the remarkable murals of Cacaxtla, in Tlaxcala, which were painted in the 7th–9th centuries AD. Artists combined concern with representing the human body in action (for example, in the Mural of the Battle in Building B) with a commitment to near-abstract scenes dense with religious symbolism (such as the murals possibly representing the sun and moon in Building A).

Artists of the Aztec era enthusiastically pursued naturalism in some statuary, but in painted work on vases and in codices followed the tradition of Teotihuacán.

The codex art of the Mixtecs and Aztecs was reminiscent of Teotihuacáno murals in representing humans in profile in flat, almost schematic scenes. It differed in that it was often focused on the recording of dynastic history and the achievements of rulers, while Teotihuacáno art was intent on celebrating fertility through religious symbols.

The murals of cities such as Tulum, Xelhá and Cobá on or near the Caribbean coast of Yucatán in the 13–16th centuries returned to the religious-artistic themes of the Teotihuacános. It used a decorative style that was close to that of the Mixtec codices to celebrate fertility and astronomic themes using images of deities and religious symbols.

Left: The evocative impact of Teotihuacáno art is evident in this jade mask, probably intended for funerary use.

INDEX

This edition is published by Hermes House

Hermes House is an imprint of
Anness Publishing Ltd
Hermes House
88–89 Blackfriars Road
London SE1 8HA
tel. 020 7401 2077
fax 020 7633 9499
info@anness.com

Publisher: Joanna Lorenz
Editorial Director: Helen Sudell
Editor: Joy Wotton
Designer: Nigel Partridge
Illustrator: Peter Bull Art Studio
Production Controller: Wendy Lawson

10 9 8 7 6 5 4 3 2 1